THE WORLD OF
THE ROCK

Written by
Steve Pantaleo

CONTENTS

INTRODUCTION

Since an early age, Dwayne "The Rock" Johnson's life has revolved around sports entertainment. Growing up with fierce competitors on all branches of his family tree, his earliest memories include watching matches with wide-eyed amazement at the famed Sportatorium in Dallas, Texas, and rubbing elbows with future WWE Hall of Famers. As he grew from a shy youngster to a prime athletic specimen, it was clear his natural gifts and the warrior blood of his ancestors would propel him to greatness. Still, few could have envisioned the incredible heights that his epic journey would take him to, and his relentless pursuit to conquer the entertainment world. From the football gridiron, to the WWE canvas, to the silver screens of Hollywood, this is THE WORLD OF THE ROCK.

The Rock heaves his biggest foe, Stone Cold Steve Austin, into a Rock Bottom (*WrestleMania XV*, March 28, 1999).

WHO IS THE ROCK?

THE ROCK 101
WHAT EVERY FAN SHOULD KNOW ABOUT DWAYNE "THE ROCK" JOHNSON...

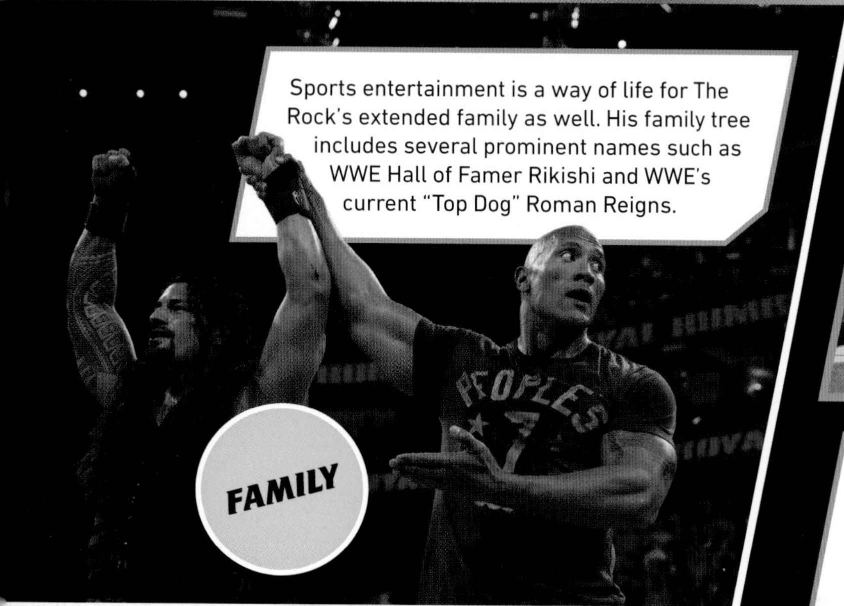

Sports entertainment is a way of life for The Rock's extended family as well. His family tree includes several prominent names such as WWE Hall of Famer Rikishi and WWE's current "Top Dog" Roman Reigns.

FAMILY

MOVIES

"The Most Electrifying Man in all of Entertainment" is no exaggeration. With starring roles in nearly 40 movies, The Rock has transcended WWE to etch his name among the Hollywood elite.

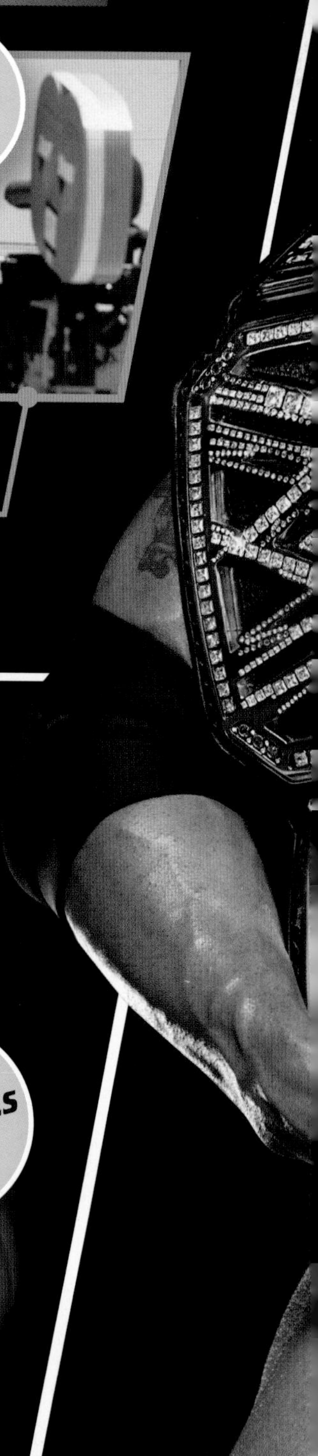

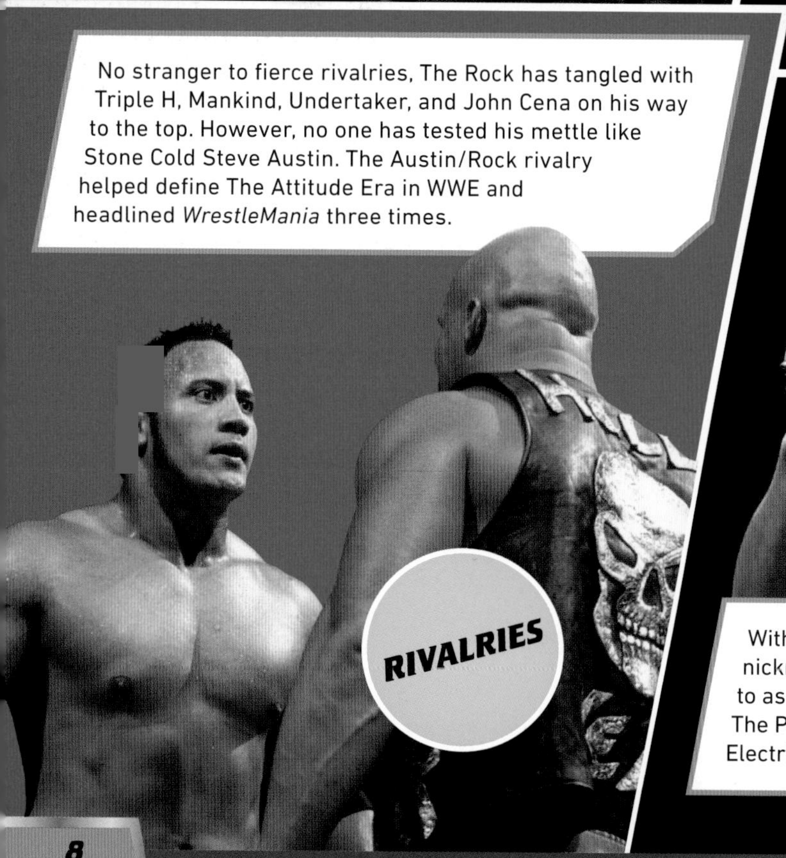

No stranger to fierce rivalries, The Rock has tangled with Triple H, Mankind, Undertaker, and John Cena on his way to the top. However, no one has tested his mettle like Stone Cold Steve Austin. The Austin/Rock rivalry helped define The Attitude Era in WWE and headlined *WrestleMania* three times.

RIVALRIES

NICKNAMES

With many talents comes many nicknames. The Rock is often referred to as The Brahma Bull, The Great One, The People's Champion, and The Most Electrifying Man in All of Entertainment.

The Rock is an eight-time WWE Champion, having achieved the fourth most reigns of all time.

LEGACY

The Rock is the first third-generation Superstar in WWE history. Both his father, Rocky Johnson, and his maternal grandfather, High Chief Peter Maivia, are WWE Hall of Famers.

The Great One lays the SmackDown both in the ring and on the microphone. His stinging putdowns and legendary catchphrases excite and de light the WWE Universe. Whether competing as an honorable hero or a rule-breaking villain, his undeniable charisma has made The Rock one of WWE's most popular stars.

The Rock's daily fitness regimen is not for jabronis. It takes intense commitment to training and nutrition to have a physique as hard as, well, a rock.

TRAINING

SMACK TALK

9

THE MAIVIA/ JOHNSON FAMILY

THE NAMES ANOA'I and Johnson are among the most revered in sports entertainment history. The family legacy began in the South Pacific island of American Samoa, where The Rock's grandfather, Peter Maivia, was born in the 1930s. While building a ring resume that would one day land him in the WWE Hall of Fame, Maivia teamed with another future legend, Rocky Johnson, who became his son-in-law and father to his electrifying grandson, Dwayne. For an unprecedented three generations, the men and women of the Maivia/Johnson family have built a legacy in WWE, one that is poised to continue for years to come.

HIGH CHIEF PETER MAIVIA

Peter Maivia began competing in the early 1960s. By the turn of the next decade, he had earned a reputation as one of the toughest men to step into the ring. Considered a Samoan High Chief in his home country, The Rock's grandfather chose the name High Chief Peter Maivia as his ring name. In keeping with Samoan traditions, the High Chief's legs and abdomen were blanketed with tattoos. This impressive body ink indicated his rank and also added to his allure with fans. The Rock later carried on this tradition, displaying similar designs on his arms, shoulders, and chest.

The High Chief shows off his incredible physique, made more imposing by a canopy of tribal tattoos.

Peter Maivia won championships in the South Pacific and Hawaii before arriving in the U.S. in 1970. Maivia soon earned more accolades, both in singles and tag team competition. He partnered with San Francisco legend Pat Patterson—who would later help recruit The Rock to WWE—to capture the NWA Tag Team Championship. WWE founder Vincent J. McMahon brought Maivia to WWE during the late 1970s. McMahon's son, current WWE Chairman Vincent K. McMahon, remembers the High Chief as "a tough S.O.B. and someone that was not to be messed with, while being a genuine and likable man away from the ring."

In the latter part of his career, Maivia displayed a mean streak. He turned on his friend, Bob Backlund, attacking him during a match. Maivia ended the friendship in order to set his sights on Backlund's WWE Championship. This instantly transformed Maivia from a fan-favorite to one of the most detested Superstars of his time. He then aligned with "Classy" Freddie Blassie, a reviled manager known for guiding the most unsavory rule-breakers in WWE, and repeatedly challenged Backlund for the WWE Championship. Despite never winning the gold, Maivia proved a top draw. Fans flocked to see him grapple with the clean-cut, popular champion, Backlund.

Away from the cameras, Maivia mentored several noteworthy stars, including Superstar Billy Graham and two eccentric WWE newcomers, his cousins Afa and Sika, The Wild Samoans. The Maivia/ Anoa'i family had sown the first seeds of its WWE dominance.

(Left to right), The Rock's grandmother Lia, mother Ata, and grandfather Peter in 1965.

Maivia married Lia Fuataga and the couple had a daughter, Ata. Years later, Maivia's younger teammate, Rocky Johnson, began a relationship with Ata. Maivia initially disapproved, concerned about the chaotic lifestyle of a sports entertainer, but Rocky and Ata eventually married; on May 2, 1972, they welcomed their son, Dwayne Johnson, into the world.

Sadly, Peter Maivia was diagnosed with cancer in 1981 and passed away the following year at the young age of 45. Following his death, his wife Lia assumed control of the NWA promotion, Polynesian Pro Wrestling, which Maivia had been in charge of, becoming one of the first-ever female promoters in the history of sports entertainment. Under her shrewd leadership, PPW produced a TV show called *Polynesian Pacific Pro Wrestling* featuring several successful live events. Throughout the 1980s, the Anoa'i/Maivia family tree further extended its roots into sports entertainment. Today, the WWE Universe remembers several illustrious careers, while the legacy continues to unfold each week on *RAW* and *SmackDown*.

The Johnson family, Rocky, Ata, and young Dwayne pose for a family photo.

ROCKY JOHNSON

The Rock's father, Rocky Johnson lands one of his famed Drop Kicks to an unfortunate foe.

Today, many people know The Rock's father, "Soul Man" Rocky Johnson, primarily for his "trailblazin', eyebrow raisin'" son Dwayne, but the elder Johnson also made a lasting impact of his own. He lit up the sports entertainment canvas with a dizzying array of athletic kip-ups, take downs, and a breathtaking drop kick that is envied in the WWE locker room to this day. Johnson's flashy footwork, chiseled physique, and charisma made him one of the most exciting Superstars of the 1970s. While competing in WWE, he partnered with Tony Atlas to form The Soul Patrol and defeated The Wild Samoans for the World Tag Team Championships. The win made them the first team of African-American Superstars to capture the titles.

Johnson's influence continued over a decade later when he trained his son. The proud father even returned to the ring to aid his son during The Rock's early matches in WWE.

> "I remember watching my dad... I wanted to have that same type of, as he would say, "razzlematazz." My dad was awesome!"
>
> **The Rock**

NIA JAX

A cousin to The Rock on the Maivia side, Nia Jax is one of the most feared Superstars in the history of the WWE women's division. With an icy glare and intimidating stature, Jax is, as her entrance theme proudly proclaims, "not like most girls." Standing six feet tall, she throws most girls around as if they were rag dolls. Having pushed around her competition on *NXT*, Jax was drafted to *RAW* in 2016. Since her arrival, top Superstars from Bayley to Sasha Banks and Alexa Bliss have fallen victim to her imposing strength. With athleticism to match her raw power, Nia Jax has all the tools to be a destructive force for years to come.

Nia Jax powers up both Sasha Banks and Alexa Bliss for an impressive double Samoan Drop (*No Mercy*, September 24, 2017).

THE ANOA'I FAMILY

PETER MAIVIA forged a special bond with another Samoan patriarch, Amituana'i Anoa'i, when he trained Amituana'i's sons, Wild Samoans Afa and Sika, for the ring. The two men took part in a sacred ritual to become "blood brothers" forming a lasting bond between the Anoa'i and Maivia clans. Though not related by birth, members of both bloodlines regard each other as family, supporting each other in and out of the ring. Together, the two family trees include six members of the WWE Hall of Fame, with The Rock a sure bet to become the seventh.

TONGA KID

Tonga Kid flashes an "I love you" hand gesture much like his ally, Jimmy Snuka.

Tonga Kid, son of The Wild Samoan's sister, Vera, joined WWE in 1983. Decked in island garb, he made an instant impression by aiding "Superfly" Jimmy Snuka in his battles with Roddy Piper. With an offense similar in style to famed Superstar Snuka's energetic in-ring action, Kid dazzled crowds with his leaping ability and high-flying moves from the top rope. Rivals included notorious villains such as Mr. Fuji, Iron Sheik, and "Mr. Wonderful" Paul Orndorff. Tonga Kid reinvented himself as Tama in 1986 and formed a tag team with Haku called The Islanders. With The Islanders, Tama became more vicious and fell under the influence of manager and notorious scoundrel Bobby "The Brain" Heenan. With Heenan guiding them, the duo took villainy to new levels, even kidnapping the British Bulldogs' canine mascot, Matilda. Shortly after the team's biggest victory over the Bulldogs at *WrestleMania IV*, Tama left WWE, effectively breaking up The Islanders.

THE WILD SAMOANS

Feared and loathed by fellow Superstars and the WWE Universe throughout the 1980s, The Wild Samoans Afa and Sika were two of the most outlandish sports entertainment stars of all time. The Wild Samoans, sons of Amituana'i Anoa'i, blood brother to Peter Maivia, were known for competing barefoot, communicating in grunts, and devouring raw fish inside the ring. Chief among their many accomplishments in the ring were three World Tag Team Championships in WWE, with title reigns totaling over a year's length. Although their active career ended decades ago, Afa and Sika's impact continues to be felt. Aside from numerous familial connections to WWE, the duo has ushered several trainees into sports entertainment from their school, The Wild Samoan Training Center. Famous pupils include Batista, Freebird Michael Hayes, Billy Kidman, and the Samoans' own sons. Afa is father to former Superstars Samu and Manu, while Sika is father to former Superstar Rosey and perennial World Championship contender Roman Reigns.

Wild Samoans Afa and Sika instill fear with their menacing demeanor.

“**I don't know how you measure the impact of the Anoa'i family. Their impact was tremendous and they are a great family, by the way. They are really close and love each other to death.**”

Vincent K. McMahon

THE HEADSHRINKERS

The Headshrinkers tag team and their manager Afa terrorize WWE Superstars in the early 1990s.

Initially dubbed The Samoan Swat Team, Tonga Kid's brother Fatu and cousin Samu came to WWE in 1992 as The Headshrinkers. Managed by Samu's father, Afa, the team were similar in style to The Wild Samoans. To psych out opponents, they gnawed on turkey carcasses and grunted wildly. They unnerved fans at first, but eventually became popular. Soon after, "Captain" Lou Albano took over as their manager and The Headshrinkers claimed their sole World Tag Team Championship, defeating The Quebecers. Albano's impact on the team was positive at first. However, the Captain's later attempts to rein in their behavior were largely unsuccessful and the partnership dissolved in 1995. Samu formed a lesser-known team with his cousin Matt Anoa'i called the Samoan Gangsta Party. However, Fatu achieved greater fame later in his WWE career as Rikishi.

RIKISHI

The lovable Rikishi (middle) dances with Too Cool partners Scotty 2 Hotty (left) and Grandmaster Sexay (right).

Following the demise of The Headshrinkers, Fatu saw some success as a masked Superstar named The Sultan, but found his groove as the fun-loving Rikishi. Showcasing his infectious dance moves and ample rear end, Rikishi aligned with a team known as Too Cool. Fans gravitated to the colorfully dressed trio, and loved their postmatch dance routines. Perhaps no maneuver in WWE history was as feared as Rikishi's Stinkface. With his opponent sitting in the corner of the ring and his signature thong on display, Rikishi would thrust his massive hindquarters directly into his foe's face. Though disgusting, the move provided a deserved comeuppance for many hated villains, including the Chairman, Mr. McMahon!

Rikishi's popularity with fans was briefly severed in 2000, when he admitted to attacking fan-favorite Superstar Stone Cold Steve Austin with a car on behalf of The Rock. Over time, however, Rikishi worked his way back into the good graces of the WWE Universe. This former Intercontinental and Tag Team Champion was inducted into the WWE Hall of Fame in 2015 by his twin sons, The Usos.

UMAGA

"The Samoan Bulldozer," Umaga rears back to strike The Miz with a dreaded Samoan Spike move (*RAW*, May 1 2006).

Nicknamed the Samoan Bulldozer, Umaga, brother of Tonga Kid and Rikishi, was a menacing combination of pure power and intense rage. Brought to WWE in 2006 by his smarmy manager Armando Alejandro Estrada, Umaga was virtually unstoppable for several months, vanquishing some of WWE's top Superstars. Not content with simply winning, he took conflicts to dangerous levels, driving his taped thumb into his opponent's larynx—a signature move called the Samoan Spike. Umaga was so dominant that Mr. McMahon handpicked him to face the powerful Superstar Bobby Lashley (selected by Donald Trump to fight on his behalf), in the Battle of the Billionaires at *WrestleMania 23*. Despite falling short against Lashley, Umaga still captured the Intercontinental Title twice in his career and scored victories over top stars such as Kane and CM Punk.

Prior to Umaga's success, he competed as Jamal in a tag team called 3-Minute Warning alongside his cousin Rosey.

YOKOZUNA

The mighty Yokozuna comes crashing down with his Banzai Drop.

The mammoth Yokozuna terrorized WWE during the 1990s, flattening several top Superstars with his devastating Banzai Drop. Although Samoan by birth, Yokozuna competed as a Japanese sumo wrestler under the guidance of the devious Mr. Fuji. His impact on the WWE landscape was instant and profound. Weighing close to 600 pounds, and immensely strong, Yokozuna also possessed surprising agility, allowing him to keep pace with anyone in the ring. Within months of his October 1992 debut, he heaved "Macho Man" Randy Savage over the top rope to win the Royal Rumble Match. In the main event of *WrestleMania IX*, he ousted Bret "Hit Man" Hart for the WWE Championship after Fuji temporarily blinded Hart with salt. Yokozuna's reign was short-lived, but his dominance was only just beginning. He defeated Hulk Hogan to recapture the gold and held the title for nearly a year, taunting challengers and spectators with his warcry, "Banzai!" The menacing big man finally earned his first cheers in 1996, when he spurned manager Jim Cornette and the hated Camp Cornette stable. Today, this Hall of Famer is fondly remembered for his ferocity in the ring and his kind-hearted nature away from it.

ROSEY

Rosey shows off his crime-fighting attire (May 16, 2005).

The 3-Minute Warning team served as goons for *RAW* General Manager Eric Bischoff. When the tyrannical GM became bored with what was transpiring on *RAW*, he gave those involved three minutes before unleashing cousins Rosey and Jamal to expel them from the ring. This gig was short-lived, but, soon after, Rosey found his true calling. After a crash course in crime fighting from WWE's resident superhero, The Hurricane, Rosey donned a mask and joined him on the quest to rid WWE of evildoers. The lovable crusaders reached their apex at *Backlash 2005*, when they toppled Cade and Murdoch for the World Tag Team Championship.

ROMAN REIGNS

Whether alongside his brothers-in-arms in The Shield or fighting his own battles, the son of Wild Samoan Sika has built his "Roman Empire" brick by brick. A man of few words, Roman prefers to let his wrecking ball of a fist do the talking. His breakout star potential was first seen in the 2014 Royal Rumble Match, where he broke the record for eliminations in a single contest. Roman followed up this performance in 2015 by going the distance and winning the 30-man melee. When The Rock, made a rare appearance to support him, it was clear that greater conquests lay ahead. Roman went on to headline the next four *WrestleManias*. He overtook the imperial Triple H at *WrestleMania 32* and, the following year, sent Undertaker into retirement, dealing the Deadman only his second loss in 25 *WrestleMania* matches. Reprising one of Undertaker's popular catchphrases, Roman proclaimed that WWE was now "his yard." Since then, whether fans love him or hate him, he has proven to be exactly what he says he is, "The Big Dog" in WWE.

Roman Reigns proudly carries on his family legacy in WWE.

THE USOS (AND NAOMI)

From day one, twin brothers Jimmy and Jey Uso lived up to their proud lineage. Sporting flashy outfits and matching face paint, the sons of Rikishi burst onto the scene in 2010. They danced the *siva tau* war dance during their entrance and commanded, "When we say 'Uce,' y'all say 'O,'" to a riled-up WWE Universe. Their stunning, high-flying displays in the ring delighted crowds and signaled trouble for rival teams such as the Hart Dynasty and The Prime Time Players. After collecting multiple tag team titles, the Usos shocked WWE in 2016 when they adopted a grittier persona, threatening to sentence rivals to the "Uso Penitentiary." This newfound nasty streak earned them plenty of jeers, but with three *SmackDown* Tag Team Championships and counting, Jimmy and Jey didn't care.

Naomi gives the *SmackDown* Women's Championship a bit of personal flair using vibrant neon lights (*SmackDown Live*, July 18, 2017).

The Usos have the *SmackDown* Tag Team championships "on lock down" (*SmackDown Live*, June 27, 2017)

Jimmy's wife, Naomi, is another *SmackDown* Superstar familiar with championships. After flying under the radar managing The Usos and others, she began to light up the *SmackDown* women's division as a competitor. Decked in eye-popping neon, Naomi captured the *SmackDown* Women's Championship at *Elimination Chamber* 2017 and then again at *WrestleMania 33*. Naomi has continued to make one-and-all "feel the glow."

THE ANOA'I AND MAIVIA FAMILY TREES

The Anoa'i and Maivia family were joined together when Amituana'i Anoa'i and Peter Maivia became "blood brothers." The two families have had a tremendous impact on sports entertainment and have produced several WWE Superstars.

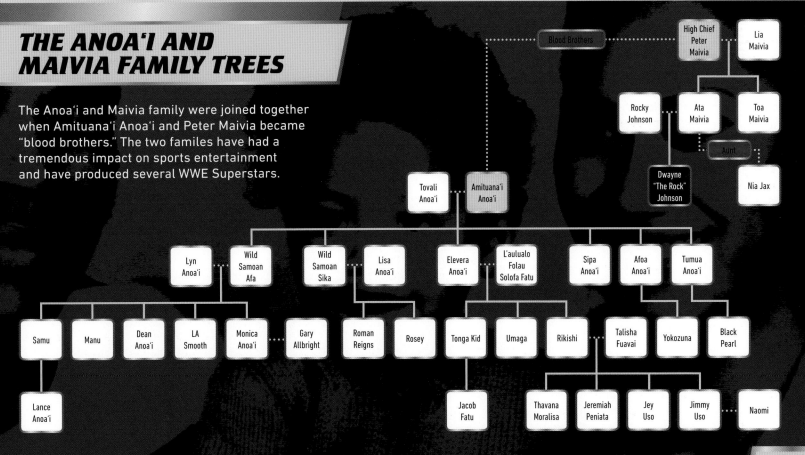

THE EVOLUTION OF THE GREAT ONE

THROUGH HIS UNENDING pursuit of greatness, The Rock has continuously reinvented himself to look every bit the champion he strives to be. From amazing body art, to glimmering outfits pricier than a car, to t-shirts bearing slogans that his legions of fans also wore, every incarnation of The People's Champ matched a change in the Superstar's approach to his burgeoning career in sports entertainment.

1998: Now called The Rock, his newfound popularity came with new ink. The Rock's iconic Brahma Bull tattoo signified his strength and defiance. It also defined his true personality, which began to surface along with his famed facial expression, the People's Eyebrow.

1997: Black trunks and accessories provided more understated attire for his lone Intercontinental Title reign as Rocky Maivia.

1996

1997

1998

1996: Rocky Maivia was all smiles for his debut at *Survivor Series 1996*. The highly touted rookie wore an intriguing ensemble with dangling ribbons and leaves alongside a mop of curly hair atop his head.

Early 1999: During his hard-hitting rivalry with Mankind, The Rock matched the more formal theme of his new faction, The Corporation, with a shirt and shades.

Mid 1999: Sporting one of the earliest of many official t-shirts, The Rock was the definition of cool in his signature shades and expensive accessories.

Late 1999: The Rock often boasted about the price of his flashy wardrobe. He owned several different-color shirts with this majestic lion design.

THE EVOLUTION OF THE GREAT ONE

Early 2000: Every Brahma Bull needs a cow. The Rock wore his as a vest. Of his many vests, this one was easily his boldest fashion statement.

Late 2000: Much of The Rock's attire is custom made. He had this button-down shirt specially designed to show off his famous bull logo.

Early 2011: After seven years away from WWE, The Rock finally came back to host *WrestleMania*. As master of ceremonies for WWE's biggest show, he looked sharp and ready to lay the smackdown.

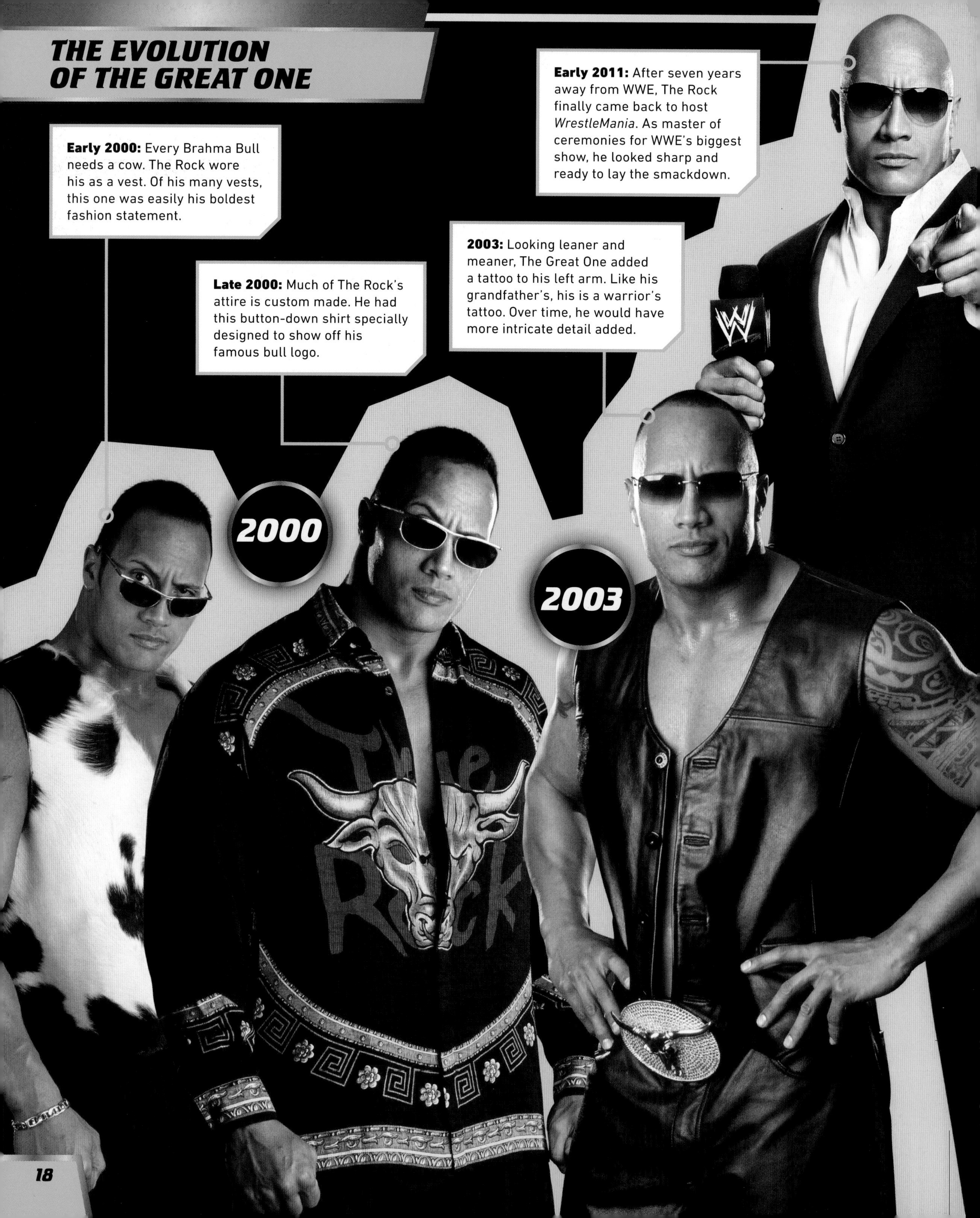

2003: Looking leaner and meaner, The Great One added a tattoo to his left arm. Like his grandfather's, his is a warrior's tattoo. Over time, he would have more intricate detail added.

2000

2003

2011

Late 2011: The Rock returned to the ring in the best shape of his life, determined to once again become WWE Champion. While away, his warrior's ink was expanded to cover his heart. It includes many symbolic tributes to his family and all he holds dear.

Early 2012: The Rock's supporters, known as "Team Bring It," rallied together to cheer on their hero against John Cena. The Rock had a "C" on his Team Bring It t-shirt to signify that he was the team's captain.

2013: Though in the best shape of his life, The Rock felt his shoulder muscles were missing something: the weight of the WWE Title! He filled this void at *Royal Rumble* and gave the title's design a long overdue makeover to fit his style.

2012

2013

PLAYING THE FOOTBALL FIELD

After a stellar high school career, Dwayne Johnson plays college football for the vaunted Miami Hurricanes. Known for their brashness as much as their success on the field, the Hurricanes win a national championship in Dwayne's freshman season.

THE ROCK DOMINATES

RAW: Now known as The Rock, the brazen Superstar overthrows Faarooq to assume leadership over his faction, The Nation of Domination.

1991 – 1994

Nov 17, 1996

Mar 30, 1998

Aug 18, 1997

A SUPER START

Survivor Series: As many of his Miami teammates predict, Dwayne Johnson becomes a WWE Superstar. He debuts at *Survivor Series 1996* as Rocky Maivia, combining the names of his father and grandfather.

JOINING FORCES WITH FAAROOQ

RAW: Maivia joins the Nation of Domination, abandoning the colorful, smiley persona that had been harshly rejected by fans.

A CORPORATE ALLIANCE
Survivor Series: WWE Chairman Mr. McMahon helps The Rock win his first WWE Championship, exposing their shocking allegiance. To the people's dismay, he becomes known as The Corporate Champion.

THE PEOPLE GET THEIR CHAMPION
RAW: Once again, The Rock's personality begins to outshine his villainous actions, causing the WWE Universe to cheer him. During a confrontation with Shane McMahon, he spilts from The Corporation, becoming The People's Champion from then on.

Nov 15, 1998

Mar 22, 1999

Apr 26, 1999

Apr 29, 1999

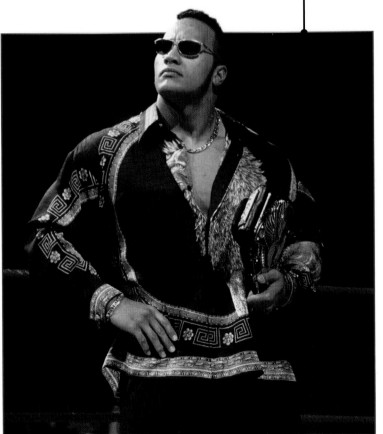

CORPORATE PERKS
RAW: The Rock wears a lavishly expensive wardrobe, flaunting his excesses earned as Mr. McMahon's "crown jewel." His polished persona makes him and the disheveled Superstar Mankind natural rivals.

SMACK-TALKIN' INTO WWE HISTORY
SmackDown: WWE debuts a new show called *SmackDown*. The name is inspired by one of The Rock's catchphrases, in which he promises to "lay the smackdown" on his foes.

AN UNEXPECTED CONNECTION
RAW: A partnership that no one, not even the two Superstars themselves, could have predicted is forged when Mankind and The Rock team together for the first time. The odd pair go on to win three Word Tag Team Titles as The Rock 'n' Sock Connection.

ROCKING THE RUMBLE
Royal Rumble: In the same building he debuted, Madison Square Garden, The Rock wins the Royal Rumble Match for the only time in his career.

Aug 30, 1999

Sep 27, 1999

Jan 5, 2000

Jan 23, 2000

THE ROCK'S LIFE ON SHOW
RAW: Mankind presents "Rock, This Is Your Life," one of the most amusing and celebrated segments in *RAW* history, featuring an eclectic mix of people from The Rock's past.

THE ROCK SAYS...
The People's Champion's first autobiography, *The Rock Says...* hits bookstores and quickly becomes a *New York Times* bestseller.

HOLLYWOOD CALLS
The Rock makes his motion picture debut in *The Mummy Returns*.

BATTLING TRIPLE H
RAW: With his career-long rivalry with Triple H at its most intense, The Rock takes out the entire McMahon-Helmsley faction.

May 1, 2000

May 22, 2000

Dec 4, 2000

May 4, 2001

Aug 19, 2001

A WIN FOR THE PEOPLE
RAW: After defeating Triple H the night before at *Backlash*, The Rock shows off his newly won WWE Championship. It is his fourth reign with the Title, but his first as a full-fledged fan-favorite.

STONE-COLD ATTITUDE
RAW: Unfazed about his upcoming Six-Man Hell in a Cell Match, The Rock performs a mocking impersonation of all five of his opponents, including his biggest rival, Stone Cold Steve Austin.

WCW CHAMPION
SummerSlam: Returning from a long absence, The People's Champ finds himself embroiled in WWE's battle against The Alliance. He scores a major win for himself and WWE when he captures the WCW Championship from The Alliance's Booker T.

ALLIANCE EXTINGUISHED
RAW: At *Survivor Series*, The Rock leads the charge to vanquish The Alliance once and for all, then triumphantly appears the next night to begin a new era with the WCW Championship.

THE ROCK RAPS
SmackDown: Hip-hop star Busta Rhymes joins The Rock in the ring to help electrify the Atlantic City crowd with a musical number.

Nov 19, 2001 **Mar 17, 2002** **Mar 25, 2002** **Jul 11, 2002**

WWE DRAFT'S TOP PICK
RAW: The Rock is selected by *SmackDown* as the first overall pick in the inaugural WWE Draft, making him the exclusive property of the show he helped to name.

ICON VS. ICON
WrestleMania X8: In an emotional match hyped as Icon vs Icon, The Rock triumphs over "Hollywood" Hulk Hogan.

A STONE COLD WIN

WrestleMania XIX: The Rock and Stone Cold Steve Austin solidify their rivalry among the greatest in history, competing against each other for the third time at *WrestleMania*. The Rock picks up his only win in the series.

UNDISPUTED CHAMP

Vengeance: For the first time since the WWE and WCW Championships were unified, The Rock enjoys a reign as Undisputed Champion.

Jul 21, 2002

Mar 30, 2003

Mar 31, 2003

Mar 29, 2008

THE ROCK VS. THE PEOPLE

RAW: Sensing animosity from the WWE Universe with his choice to branch out into Hollywood, The Great One responds by hurling insults at crowds, becoming a villain for the first time in four years.

FAMILY FAME

WWE Hall of Fame Induction Ceremony: Making a rare appearance in front of the WWE Universe, The Rock gives an entertaining speech inducting both his father and grandfather into the WWE Hall of Fame.

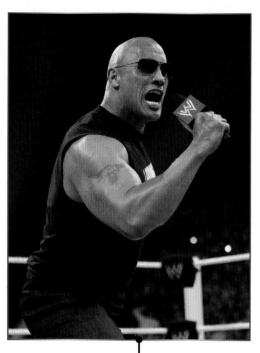

THE ROCK RETURNS

RAW: The Rock appears in person on WWE programming for the first time in seven years. Bringing back his vintage microphone skills, he lays the groundwork for a new era for himself and WWE.

ROCK CONCERTS

RAW 20th Anniversary: An anniversary bash calls for the return of the "Rock Concert," a reoccurring section where The Rock uses his musical prowess to insult his rivals. This time, he parodies Eric Clapton's "Wonderful Tonight," serenading unpopular General Manager Vickie Guerrero with the chorus, *"You look horrible tonight."*

Feb 14, 2011

Apr 1, 2012

Jan 14, 2013

ONCE IN A LIFETIME

WrestleMania XXVIII: In front of his home city of Miami, The Rock beats John Cena in what it is widely considered the most anticipated match of all time.

AN EIGHTH REIGN
Royal Rumble: Ten years removed from his last WWE Championship reign, The Rock defeats CM Punk to reclaim the title for the eighth time.

THE PEOPLE'S HEARTTHROB
With innumerable Hollywood credits and awards already attached to his name, Dwayne Johnson received yet another when he was named *People* Magazine's "Sexiest Man Alive."

Jan 27, 2013

Dec 18, 2013

Nov 28, 2016

Dec 13, 2017

STAR RECOGNITION
Dwayne Johnson receives a star on the Hollywood Walk of Fame bearing his name, an honor reserved for the most elite among A-list entertainers.

HOLLYWOOD RETURNS
Twelve years after his first film, *The Mummy Returns*, Dwayne "The Rock" Johnson is named the top grossing actor in the world by *Forbes Magazine* for the first time.

Photo courtesy of Hollywood Chamber of Commerce.

The Rock salutes 76,976 adoring fans in Santa Clara at *WrestleMania 31*.

THE ROCK'S CATCHPHRASES

ASIDE FROM THE many official accolades he has collected, The Rock is widely regarded as the greatest trash-talker in WWE history. His catchphrases and putdowns give his appearances the feel of a rock concert, as the exuberant crowd echoes his words back to him.

"**The people are chanting** The Rock's name..."

Often used to hush a pesky interviewer or opponent, this is an authoritative reminder to zip one's lip so the people can properly express their adoration.

"Finally, The Rock has **come back** to (insert host city)!"

This customary greeting forges a special connection, virtually making him an honorary citizen of the host city for that night.

The Rock electrifies the *RAW* crowd with his biting comebacks (March 31, 2003).

"Know your **role** and shut your **mouth!**"

This iconic demand for silence was inspired by many long car rides with The Nation of Domination. Ron Simmons (a.k.a. Faarooq) often told others to "know their role." The Rock took his stablemate's expression and made it legendary.

The Rock tells John Cena to "just bring it" (*RAW*, March 25, 2013).

"Just bring it!"

The Rock's fans became known as "Team Bring It" to pay homage to this famous taunt.

"You will go one on one with The Great One!"

Sometimes the wicked need a firm reminder of what they are up against. Hearing this out loud sends a shudder down the spine of the most ruthless villains set to face The Great One in the ring.

"Shine it up real nice, flip it sideways..."

No matter the object, The Rock gave vivid detail of just how he planned to stick it back to his opponents.

"The Rock says..."

Though it is emphatically clear who is talking, prefacing his statement with a third-person quote attribution drives home The Rock's point.

"It doesn't matter!"

Often regarded as the most epic burn a Superstar can receive, "It doesn't matter" works with any question. Most commonly, The Rock will ask someone what they think or what their name is, then rudely interrupt them before they can answer, leaving them tongue-tied.

The Rock waits for the precise moment to interrupt his foe (*RAW*, July 11, 1999).

"Take a right at the end of **Jabroni Drive**, and check right into the **SmackDown Hotel!**"

Rivals can say what they will about him, but at least The Great One is courteous enough to give them explicit directions to their eventual defeat.

"The Rock will lay **the smackdown** on ALL your candy asses!"

Thanks to this eternal threat, The Rock is the only Superstar in history to get a WWE show named in his honor. In 1999, *SmackDown* made its debut and the show battles *RAW* for brand supremacy to this day. When circumstances called for a beating of Shakespearian gravitas, the phrase was tweaked to "layeth the smackethdown."

Big Show is dismissed as a "sick freak" (*RAW*, March 2, 1999).

"Who in the **blue hell** are you?"

The jury is out as to whether the blue hell is worse than the regular kind, but this trademark retort tells opponents they are too insignificant for The Rock to know who they are.

"**You sick ffffreak!**"

The Rock uses this phrase to express his bewilderment toward unsavory or bizarre behaviors by his peers.

"The millions **(and millions!)** of The Rock's fans!"

The Rock's dramatic pause after the first "millions" allows for the crowd to chime in.

"No one...
**and The
Rock means...**
no one..."

A bold statement, The Brahma Bull likes to emphasize that no one can get between him and his goal.

"The **jabroni** beatin', (la la la la laow!) **pie** eatin', trail blazin', **eyebrow** raisin', heart stoppin', **elbow** droppin', People's Champ, The Rock!"

Brought to the WWE lexicon by the Iron Sheik, "jabroni" is a putdown that implies a rival is either soft, a wimp, or some other undesirable quality. Punctuated by his "La, la, la, la laow" tongue flick, this retort is reminiscent of trash-talking pioneers such as Ric Flair, Dusty Rhodes, and "Superstar" Billy Graham.

"If ya **smeeeeellllll** what The Rock is cookin'!"

This final send-off gives the WWE Universe one more chance to explode before The Rock departs to electrify the next city.

The Rock isn't short on words upon his long-awaited return to WWE (*RAW*, February 14, 2011).

SIGNATURE MOVES
ROCK BOTTOM

THE DEFINITION OF Rock Bottom is the lowest possible limit. For opponents of The Rock, that is exactly what the move is. Like Steve Austin's Stone Cold Stunner and Shawn Michaels' Sweet Chin Music, the Rock Bottom meets all the requirements of a legendary finisher. The swift side slam has both ignited epic rivalries and settled them once and for all. It has spelled the beginning of over a dozen championship reigns and a dreaded comeuppance for many competitors—not to mention the destruction of several announcers' tables. For fans, there is no higher point of elation than seeing a competitor slammed to the mat as an announcer screams, "Rock Bottom! Rock Bottom!"

Chris Jericho feels the brunt of a powerful Rock Bottom (*RAW*, November 26, 2001)

Over the years, fans have debated which of The Rock's primary signature moves, the Peoples' Elbow or Rock Bottom, is his true finisher. The answer? It doesn't matter! Both bring the WWE Universe to a fever pitch and both assure The Rock leaves the ring with his hand raised in triumph. The People's Elbow has been dubbed, "The Most Electrifying Move in All of Sports Entertainment," while the Rock Bottom has had a WWE event named after it and has even appeared on the silver screen. In the 2017 movie *Furious 7*, The Rock's character, Luke Hobbs, sends his co-star Jason Statham crashing through a glass table, exactly 20 years after The Rock first unveiled the move on the Superstar D-Lo Brown during an episode of *RAW*.

Rock hard

The Rock began to fine tune his range of manuevers as he evolved from the smiling Rocky Maivia into the defiant Superstar who captured the hearts of millions. His elaborate moves were showcased at opportune moments, which built excitement in the Superstar's appearances. When given an opening, he applied the Rock Bottom by driving his shoulder up and under that of his opponent. This leverage allowed him to hoist a man of any size off his feet. Once elevated, The Rock tipped forward and broke his fall with his free arm while his horrified opponent landed flat on the mat with a match-ending thud.

The Rock performs one of the first-ever Rock Bottoms on Savio Vega (April 20, 1997).

THE GREATEST ROCK BOTTOMS

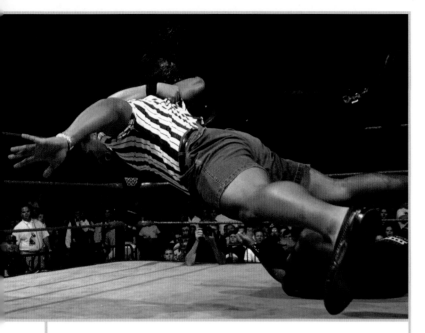

D-Von! Get the ice pack!
October 1, 2001 (*RAW*): Outnumbered and facing both Dudley Boyz in their signature Tables Match, The Rock was in danger of losing the WCW Championship. Thankfully, he persevered and gave Bubba Ray a taste of his own medicine, smashing him through a table.

Who sucks now?
August 11, 1997 (*RAW*): After hearing the WWE Universe chant "Rocky Sucks," the young Rocky Maivia decided to return the hate. During a match with Nation of Domination faction leader Faarooq and Chainz, the referee was injured. Maivia ran in to check on the referee, or so it seemed. He planted Chainz with a Rock Bottom instead and raised his fist alongside Faarooq, revealing his allegiance to the contentious faction, The Nation.

In your face!
October 16, 2001 (*SmackDown*): Many people imitate The Rock's "Just Bring It" hand gesture, but Chris Jericho is one of precious few to do so right in The Rock's face while he is talking. Jericho's audacity was commendable, but it still earned him a lovely view of the arena lights.

Well, that stinks...
October 11, 1999 (*RAW*): Symbolizing their feelings toward the British Bulldog, The Rock and his tag teammate Mankind brought a tray of bulldog excrement to the ring. During the ensuing tag team match, the feces made its way onto the mat and cushioned Bulldog's landing in the grossest possible way!

Chairman of the floored
November 9, 1998 (*RAW*): After being slapped by WWE Chairman Mr. McMahon, Rocky's intense glare alone could have sent a lesser man to the canvas. This marked the first, but not the last, time the boss would be Rock Bottomed in his own ring.

Auto abuse

December 14, 1998 (*RAW*): A powerful Rock Bottom caused more just a sore back for Mankind during a backstage brawl between Mankind and The Corporation. The Rock used Mankind to dent the hood of a fancy car.

Mirror manuevers

August 19, 2001 (*SummerSlam*): Booker T believed his signature Bookend move was superior to the very similar Rock Bottom. Not on this night. As Booker was showboating with a Spin-a-roonie dance move, The Rock kipped up and "Bottomed him out" to claim the WCW Championship.

Anything you can do...

March 19, 2012 (*RAW*): John Cena wowed the WWE Universe by heaving the 400-pound Mark Henry into an Attitude Adjustment. Not to be outdone, The Rock strutted down the ramp to perform his own powerful finisher on the behemoth.

Let's make it a double

April 30, 2000 (*Backlash*): Standing atop the Spanish announcers table, The Rock corralled Triple H and Shane McMahon into his grasp and lowered them both through the ringside furniture simultaneously with an unprecedented double Rock Bottom!

Still got it

January 25, 2015 (*Royal Rumble*): Any move that takes the 450-pound Big Show off his feet is worthy of inclusion on an all-time greatest list. The World's Largest Athlete was shocked to see his old rival and dismayed to learn he still wasn't too heavy for The People's Champ.

SIGNATURE MOVES
PEOPLE'S ELBOW

IF ANY SUPERSTAR could take a maneuver as mundane as an elbow drop and create sports entertainment gold, it is The Rock. That is exactly what happened in late 1997 and early 1998, as he was just beginning to unleash his inner Great One. The early performances of the People's Elbow were quite rudimentary, nothing like the spectacle seen today. WWE cameras did not pull back for a wide shot that captures the full power of the move. The Rock did not fling his elbow pads into a delirious audience and commentators simply described the move in the most basic terms as "a big elbow to the sternum." This is because the move was never intended to be the perennial crowd pleaser it soon became.

A powerful People's Elbow keeps Undertaker down for the count (*RAW*, June 8, 1999).

The People's Elbow was first unveiled during a non-televised live event. It was initially a routine move that was meant to be seen and quickly forgotten by a few thousand attendees. According to legend, The Rock's theatrical movements were done as a challenge to make Undertaker laugh. Whether he cracked The Deadman's grim disposition is unknown but amazingly, the quirky move earned a noisy response from the crowd. Seizing the opportunity to build on the interest, The Rock unveiled the elbow on television, running back and forth and posing dramatically before lowering his elbow. As a villain, his exaggerated hype for this simple move was meant to draw the ire of fans, but when the people applauded it, the People's Elbow became a very real terror for opponents.

Giving the people the elbow

Over time, new elements were added for additional flair: sweeping kicks to center his fallen opponent in the ring, a deliberate stomp to the mat for added noise, and a Frisbee toss of the elbow pad into the stadium seats. Not since the charismatic Superstar "Macho Man" Randy Savage delivered his version from the top turnbuckle had a basic elbow drop caused so much pandemonium. These days, the People's Elbow is a rare treat, reserved for times when WWE needs some high-voltage thrills.

The Rock drops one of the first-ever electrifying People's Elbows on Dude Love (*RAW*, November 17, 1997).

Stylin', profilin', and electrifyin'

March 14, 2004 (*WrestleMania XX*): Using an opponent's finisher against him is the ultimate show of disrespect. As "Nature Boy" Ric Flair attempted a People's Elbow of his own, The Rock sprang to his feet and flattened him. He then imitated Flair's signature strut before delivering the real thing.

Risky business

September 30, 1999 (*SmackDown*): Black dress shoes might be a poor choice to wear on a WWE mat, but their slippery soles provided a glide worthy of a Hollywood dance-off during this match. As The Rock approached a downed British Bulldog, he slid as if on skis, striking a pose as commentator Jerry Lawler howled his approval.

People's Elbow takes down People Power

March 29, 2013 (*SmackDown*): A looming *WrestleMania* rematch between The Rock and John Cena can only mean an appearance from... John Laurinaitis?! The reviled former WWE executive had been fired several months prior. The architect of the self-serving leadership style ironically named "People Power" offered to assist The Great One. To the people's delight, a "Big Johnny" resurgence was harshly rebuffed.

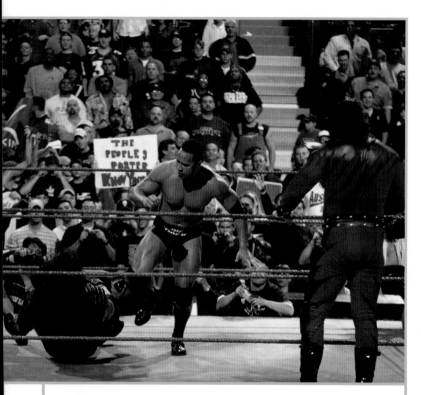

Deadman down

October 12, 1998 (*RAW*): Undertaker attempted his trademark sit-up, which usually means he has found his second wind. Not this time. The Rock stopped in mid-elbow to kick The Deadman back down, and then finished the maneuver.

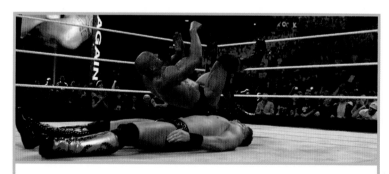

You still got it!

November 20, 2011 (*Survivor Series*): With The Miz and R-Truth spreading their hateful agenda across WWE, John Cena and The Rock agreed to a one-time partnership to silence them. The WWE Universe was treated to their hero's first ring action in seven years as the Madison Square Garden faithful came unglued to see this most electrifying move put the loudmouth Miz down for the count.

Have a nice day!
July 3, 2000 (*RAW*): Pairing with Mankind as The Rock 'n' Sock Connection, The People's Champ often let his eccentric partner in on the fun. In a particularly dynamic match, both men dropped simultaneous elbows on a fallen opponent.

An electrifying birthday
May 2, 2011 (*RAW*): Though he prefers pie over cake, The Rock still enjoys his birthday. Celebrating in his hometown of Miami, he delighted locals when he made the obnoxious Michael Cole pay for wearing the jersey of Miami's basketball rival the Boston Celtics. He then threw up the hand gesture of his alma matter the Miami Hurricanes, also known as "The U."

Record-breaking elbow
April 3, 2016 (*WrestleMania 32*): Only The Great One could deliver the exciting news that WWE had broken its own attendance record at *WrestleMania*. When Bray Wyatt interrupted him, seeking a fight, The Rock was not pleased. He silenced Wyatt in appropriate fashion, as more than 101,000 fans roared with approval.

OTHER WINNING MOVES

Sharpshooter
While not known as a submission move specialist, The Rock has mastered this legendary hold. Popularized by Hall of Famer Bret "Hit Man" Hart, the Sharpshooter puts unbearable pressure on an opponent's legs and lower back, forcing them to tap out in submission.

Spinebuster
Often used as the set-up for a People's Elbow, the Spinebuster is like a tackle in football. The Rock simply squats down, lifts his opponent by the legs, and slams him backward to the mat.

The Rock sets up a match-winning People's Elbow before slamming down on The Miz (*Survivor Series*, 2011).

THE ROCK'S
EARLY YEARS

THE "U"

BEFORE THERE WAS THE ROCK, there was "Dewey." That is what teammates called Dwayne when he was a member of the Miami Hurricanes. "Dewey" patrolled the defensive line for four years on one of college football's most memorable teams. Though he did not win fame for his time on the gridiron, many of the electrifying qualities that have shaped him as an entertainer stem from his brief football career. The rough and tumble sport helped him to harness his aggression and set him on the path to greatness.

Dwayne Johnson takes down Florida State quarterback Charlie Ward. Doak Campbell Stadium (October 9, 1993).

Growing up in a wrestling family, young Dwayne Johnson was often a target for other boys looking to prove their toughness. Never one to back down, Dwayne found himself in numerous scrapes, often leading to brushes with authority. By the time he enrolled at Freedom High School in Bethlehem, Pennsylvania—his fourth school in three years—he had developed a sizable chip on his shoulder. In his second week, he strolled into the teachers' lounge to use the bathroom, paying no heed to a male teacher's rebukes. Something about the teacher struck a chord, however, and Dwayne later sought him out to apologize. The teacher, Jody Cwik, happened to be the football coach.

"That was the day that changed everything," The Rock told *Sports Illustrated* in December 2016. Cwik offered him a spot on the team and quickly became the strong male influence that was missing in Dwayne's life, while his father traveled the world wrestling. Football became Dwayne's passion, giving his life purpose, and instilling him with the drive he is known for today. It also provided a way to win a college scholarship. Standing at 6ft 4in (1.93m) and 230 pounds (104kg), Dwayne attracted interest from several major programs, but only one team truly captivated him: the Miami Hurricanes.

Talking trash
Cocky, showy, and full of swagger, the Hurricanes' bravado earned them national attention, equally loved by supporters and reviled by opposing fans. Their emergence transformed the tranquil University of Miami into an epicenter of controversy known simply as "The U." Johnson relished the team's in-your-face mentality. With "The U," he began to master the artful brand of trash-talk that would later define The Rock persona.

Sixteen-year-old Dwayne Johnson shows off a hard-fought football trophy after playing for Freedom High School. Pennsylvania (circa 1988).

"The [trash-talk] was an art form," says The Rock. "It never stopped, and it was creative." The Hurricane's nonstop jaw-jacking intimidated opponents, and they backed up their words on the field. Johnson joined a star-studded roster that included future NFL standouts Kevin Williams, Leon Searcy, Darryl Williams, and Jessie Armstead. Their 1991 team ran roughshod over the competition, finishing undefeated and winning the NCAA National Championship. Johnson was one of the few freshmen to earn playing time.

Miami's coaches and teammates were impressed by his explosive strength and tenacity. Dwayne might have become a star player, but untimely injuries and a future football legend derailed his plans. Warren Sapp joined "The U" in 1992 as a tight end, but soon converted to defensive line, Dwayne's position group. Sapp's presence limited his playing time, forcing Dwayne to rotate in and out of the lineup.

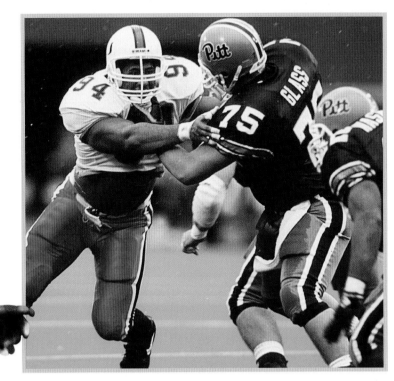

Dwayne Johnson shoves back Pitt lineman Tim Glass. Pitt Stadium (November 6, 1993).

Despite the reduced role, Johnson's versatility and work ethic impressed both coaches and teammates, including Warren Sapp himself. Dwayne appeared in 39 games in a utility role, stopping ball-carriers in their tracks and harassing opposing quarterbacks. He collected 78 tackles and four sacks in his college career. Those who saw him up close say his impact was greater than his statistics show.

Decision time

To Dwayne's great disappointment, however, no NFL team selected him in the NFL Draft. After a brief stint in the Canadian Football League, he was then cut by the Calgary Stampeders. With his football dreams dashed and just seven dollars in his pocket, he returned home. However, this rejection only made Dwayne more determined to succeed. If the door to football stardom seemed to be closing, he resolved to kick down another. He would follow his legendary family's traditions and train for a career in sports entertainment.

"He was our do-everything guy. He could play inside and out, he could play all four positions."

Pro Football Hall of Famer Warren Sapp to ESPN in 2012

The Rock returned home to Miami sporting a Hurricanes jersey adorned with his new name and old number: 94 (*RAW*, December 24, 2001.)

Dwayne Johnson shows off his speed and tenacity for the Hurricanes (circa 1994).

EARLY TRAINING

DWAYNE JOHNSON LEFT football behind to begin a new chapter. Determined to follow in his family's footsteps, he began training for a career in sports entertainment. It did not take long for the more astute minds in WWE to realize that he was a megastar in the making.

WWE legend Pat Patterson and The Rock share a moment prior to a WWE event (early 2000s).

When Dwayne informed his father, former WWE standout Rocky Johnson, of his new career path, Rocky was reluctant at first, knowing full well the toll that the physicality and nonstop travel of the WWE lifestyle takes on a person. However, he eventually agreed to teach his son the basics. Rocky did not go easy on Dwayne. He was determined to give his son a real taste of how intense and unforgiving a life in the ring could be. The Rock recalls: "I started training in Tampa, Florida, and I learned how to wrestle in a boxing ring. It was a very small, 16x16-foot ring that had no give on the mat. There was a lot of wood under the canvas, so everything hurt. So, that was a nice way to cut my teeth, by learning in a ring that was just as solid as a concrete floor." By comparison, his first bumps on a WWE mat, while still harsh, would feel like a pillow. To get there, he decided to reach out to Pat Patterson, a former tag team partner of his grandfather's and a close confidant of Vince McMahon.

Advice from the best

Following an illustrious career in the ring, Pat Patterson became a top creative advisor to the WWE Chairman. He brought in several innovations, such as the Royal Rumble Match, which helped grow WWE into the worldwide powerhouse it is today. He was also renowned for his remarkable eye for talent, and remembers seeing something special in young Dwayne. "I was living in Tampa and I got a phone call," says Pat. "This guy says, 'Is this Pat Patterson?' I said, 'Yeah.' He said, 'This is Dwayne Johnson.' Dwayne Johnson? It had been so many years, I had no idea who he was. He says, 'Rocky Johnson's son.' I said, 'My God! I haven't seen you since you were about 14 years old.' He said, 'I'd like to talk to you about wrestling.'"

Pat met Dwayne in a restaurant parking lot and was immediately impressed by his star quality. The following day, he placed a call to Vince McMahon and convinced him to fly Dwayne to Connecticut for a tryout. Upon hearing that he could potentially have the first-ever third-generation star in WWE, Vince was eager to see what skills the youngster could bring to the table. "I was brought up to Stamford, Connecticut," remembers The Rock. "And I spent a lot of time in a ring, in a warehouse with Tom Prichard." An accomplished competitor throughout the 1980s and early 90s, Prichard was also a trainer for WWE. "We would work our asses off, and I appreciate that so much, the time, the effort that Tom put in, because I love the business. I love working. I love being in the ring and trying all these new moves. I'd wake up every morning, 'Tom, I've got this idea. I'm going to stand up on this top rope and I, at 280 pounds, am going to do a backflip and land right on your chest. Want to try it?' That was a lot of fun with Tom."

Jim Ross was not just a WWE commentator but also played an important role recruiting and signing Superstars in the 1990s.

Signing a future champ

WWE Hall of Famer Jim Ross was in charge of recruiting and signing talent during this time, and recalls being highly impressed. "He had great agility, quickness. It looked like he had an aptitude for the physical part of the business. Then, the important aspect of meeting Dwayne was actually sitting down and conversing, finding out what kind of individual he was. You want to get to know the whole person. When I finally sat and talked to Rock, I knew that we had found someone that was going to be very special. If he stayed engaged, like I perceived he would, then he could be one of the greatest of all-time." WWE was in Dwayne's blood and it showed. The budding prospect showed enough athleticism, had a winning attitude, and asked all the right questions, but he was still raw. He was sent to hone his craft in Memphis, Tennessee, in a regional promotion with a history of funneling quality talent into WWE big-time. Dwayne Johnson packed his bags for his next stop, the United States Wrestling Association.

Tom Prichard helped many WWE Superstars from The Rock's generation elevate their skills in the ring.

Weeks before his big WWE debut, Rocky Maivia trains inside a WWE facility in Stamford, Connecticut (October 24, 1996).

BLUE CHIPPER

AT 23 YEARS OLD, with no bank account in his name, Dwayne Johnson drove a truck over 1,000 miles to Memphis, Tennessee, and joined Jerry Lawler's United States Wrestling Association (USWA). Lacking money for a hotel, Johnson was fortunate to find an elderly couple gracious enough to rent him a room in their house. The Rock remembers driving each day past the world-famous Sun Records, where music icons Elvis Presley, Jerry Lee Lewis, and Johnny Cash recorded their early material.

> "In a weird way, driving by that studio every day kept me motivated to stay grinding."
>
> **The Rock**

Rocky Maivia arrives ready for action in his *RAW* debut (November 18, 1996).

One of the last surviving regional sports entertainment promotions, USWA was a frequent stepping stone for budding Superstars hoping to make it to WWE. Johnson, assuming a Hawaiian persona named Flex Kavana, was determined to be the next to break into the big time. For his first professional match, he teamed with Lawler's son Brian Christopher against Lawler and Bill Dundee and won by disqualification. Despite Lawler's quips that his haircut "made him look like a pineapple," the charisma and talent of a future megastar were clearly bubbling just beneath the surface. Flex Kavana's interviews, complete with Rock-style sunglasses, were engaging and his athletic ability was staggering. Johnson's stint in USWA was brief. The rookie possessed skill beyond his years in the ring and was ready for a shot in WWE. He became the first third-generation Superstar in the company's history, taking the name Rocky Maivia, combining the names of his father and grandfather. At first, he resisted the name, determined to succeed based on his own merits rather than his lineage. WWE Chairman Vince McMahon saw it differently, however, and convinced his new recruit that his story was special and should be honored.

Survival skills

The WWE Universe saw Rocky Maivia in action for the first time at *Survivor Series* on November 17, 1996. He flashed a beaming smile and strode down the Madison Square Garden ramp in a flashy outfit that combined Samaon and Hawaiian themes. The ensemble was complete with tights, knee, and elbow pads in a jarring shade of blue with matching ribbons dangling from a neck sash. He joined Marc Mero's squad in a Traditional 4-on-4 *Survivor Series* Elimination Match. Commentators were quick to hype the newcomer as a "Blue Chipper," touting his famous bloodline. In his stellar debut match, he overcame a two-on-one disadvantage in the closing minutes to claim victory for his team.

Rocky Maivia battles Jerry "The King" Lawler (*Survivor Series*, November 17, 1996).

BLUE CHIPPER

"22,000 people did something in this moment that defined my career and literally changed my life, in one night," says The Rock. "And that thing was 22,000 people started chanting my name." Soon after, Maivia became the youngest Intercontinental Champion in WWE history. He went on to successfully defend the Championship at *WrestleMania 13* against The Sultan and, with the help of his father, Rocky Johnson, turn the tables on a postmatch attack by The Sultan's nefarious followers.

Rocky Maivia heaves The Sultan into a belly-to-belly suplex (*WrestleMania 13*, March 23, 1997).

New Intercontinental Champion Rocky Maivia proudly struts with the title around his waist (early 1997).

Although father and son fighting side-by-side was a special moment, the positive vibes for Rocky Maivia quickly came to a screeching halt. He continued to rack up wins, but as the rookie continued to smile and play by the rules, he rubbed spectators the wrong way. The encouraging chants from Maivia's debut soon became scornful chants of "Rocky sucks" and "Die Rocky Die."

A frustrated Maivia brushes off scornful jeers from the WWE Universe (*RAW*, August 8, 1997).

"Damn, I am busting my ass out there," remembers The Rock, "and they are booing me." The jeers from the stands became impossible to ignore. While taking some time off that summer to heal from an injury, the frustrated Superstar decided an attitude change was needed. If the WWE Universe wanted to hate him, why not give them a reason to?

Rocky Maivia defeats Salvatore Sincere for his first singles win (*RAW*, November 25, 1996).

BECOMING ROCKY MAIVIA

The WWE archives are full of sketches known as concept art. Concept art of Rocky Maivia was created by designers within WWE's creative department in order to illustrate the vision for the new Superstar and his signature look. Like all Superstars, artwork is based on direction from Mr. McMahon, his top advisors, and the Superstar himself. Once perfected, Superstars can acquire the proper gear and put the finishing touches on their persona.

Early Rocky Maivia sketches were done in multiple color schemes. Rocky Maivia opted for a blue/aqua combo to give a more island-themed look.

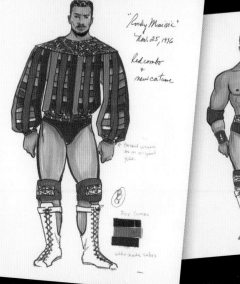

The Nation (left to right, Kama, The Rock, D-Lo Brown, and Faarooq) is incensed when they are interupted by D.O.A. (*RAW*, August 18, 1997)

ALLIES
THE NATION OF DOMINATION

DURING THE SUMMER of 1997, an injured Rocky Maivia had time to dwell on his frustration with the negative crowd reactions he had received. To get his career back on track, he decided to fight fire with fire. He aligned with The Nation of Domination, a militant faction led by Faarooq. The Nation was known for using blindsided attacks and outnumbering rivals. Upon his return in August, Maivia attacked Faarooq's opponent Chainz with a Rock Bottom and then symbolically raised his fist beside his new leader. In one swift action, the clean-cut "Blue Chipper" had become a memory.

The following week, The Nation's newest member offered no apologies for this change in attitude. He put the blame squarely on the shoulders of the heckling WWE Universe: "I got three words, 'Die Rocky Die,'" said Maivia, referencing the harsh chants he had endured for several months. "That's the gratitude I get from you pieces of crap!" This blistering tirade threw the fans' scorn back in their faces. Each week, he let loose a barrage of insults, calling fans and popular Superstars "jackasses" and shouting them down with orders to "Shut your mouth!" With his new, defiant swagger, he abandoned his original ring name and took to speaking in the third-person, calling himself "The Rock."

"I am a lot of things,
but I promise you, 'sucks'
is not one of them."

The Rock

(Left to right) Kama, Faarooq, D-Lo Brown, and The Rock as The Nation of Domination (October 1997).

ORIGINAL MEMBERS

Faarooq
The founder of The Nation of Domination who recruited likeminded Superstars to his cause until he was overthrown by The Rock.

Savio Vega
Before Faarooq fired him in May 1997, Savio rivaled future member Rocky Maivia. He later formed the Latin stable, Los Boricuas.

Clarence Mason
An attorney known for manipulating rulings in his clients' favor, Mason was the legal eagle the Nation needed outside the ring.

D-Lo Brown
Known for a chest protector that many felt gave him an unfair advantage, D-Lo was a European Champion while in The Nation.

PG-13
Consisting of rappers JC Ice and Wolfie D, PG-13 helped spread the team's threatening messages through hip-hop lyrics.

Crush
This hardnosed Superstar joined with his manager, Clarence Mason. After he was fired, he founded Disciples of Apocalypse.

OTHER MEMBERS

Kama
An asset in battles against D.O.A and Loa Boricuas in 1997, Kama left the group for more hedonistic pleasures as The Godfather.

Owen Hart
A decorated Superstar, Hart joined in 1998 and shared leadership duties with The Rock before The Nation dissolved.

Ahmed Johnson
After a brief, injury-plagued stint in 1997, Johnson was callously dismissed by his stablemates and replaced by The Rock.

Mark Henry
A champion power lifter, Henry sided with The Rock in his leadership coup. He later formed a tag team with D-Lo Brown.

The Rock becomes more vocal during his lengthy Intercontinental Championship reign (December, 1997 to August 1998).

Dominating The Nation

What Faarooq failed to realize was that he had recruited his own successor. The more The Rock berated the WWE Universe, the more they hung on his every word. During this period in WWE history, now known as The Attitude Era, fans had stopped gravitating to role-model heroes who lectured people to "say their prayers and take their vitamins," as Hulk Hogan did in the 1980s. Brash, irreverent antiheroes were what the people wanted. The Rock's new edgy disposition and seemingly endless supply of witty catchphrases and one-liners captivated fans. Not surprisingly, The Rock put his nominal leader Faarooq in the shade.

The Rock's second Intercontinental Championship reign earned him more attention. He now rivaled former MMA star Ken Shamrock, who was billed as the "World's Most Dangerous Man," as well as another force of nature, Stone Cold Steve Austin. Seeing how fast Rocky's star was rising, Faarooq became jealous and a brawl broke out between the two stablemates.

The Rock has trouble avoiding a brutal Ankle Lock from one of his first rivals, Ken Shamrock.

"The Rock is not only the leader of The Nation of Domination, he's the ruler of The Nation of Domination."

The Rock

The Rock overthrows the Nation leader Faarooq and rubs salt in his wounds with a few pointed words (*RAW*, March 30, 1998).

At the May 1998 *Over the Edge* pay-per-view, Faarooq challenged his former protégé for the Intercontinental Title, to finally settle who was the faction's true kingpin. The Rock emerged the winner, ending whatever glimmer of doubt that remained that The Nation had a new shot-caller. The group shifted its focus away from infighting to retaining the Title. They brought in champion powerlifter Mark Henry and veteran Superstar Owen Hart to aid their cause. In addition, The Rock redesigned the Intercontinental Title with a new hip design.

The Nation vs. DX

Standing in the Intercontinental Champ's way was D-Generation X (DX, for short), another controversial group and a mainstay of The Attitude Era. Both groups wanted to extinguish the other. DX had undergone a similar change in leadership, with Triple H taking over from Shawn Michaels, while Triple H had his eyes on The Rock's title. Following a summer of trading stinging insults and some all-out brawls, both groups remained intact, but cracks in The Nation had begun to develop. The Rock's unstoppable rise in popularity was causing friction with other members. Rather than peacefully go their separate ways, members D-Lo Brown and Mark Henry attacked The Rock on an October episode of *RAW*.

After The Rock pinned Henry on *RAW* in November of 1998, The Rock officially left The Nation in the rear-view mirror. By then, his boastful nickname of "The People's Champion" had become a self-fulfilling prophecy. The Rock was ready for greater conquests. With the people fully behind him, he turned the "People's Eyebrow" toward the next goal, the WWE Championship.

A brawl between The Rock and Mark Henry seals the dissolution of The Nation (*RAW*, November 3, 1998).

RIVALRIES
D-GENERATION X

THE EXPLOSIVE RIVALRY between The Nation of Domination and D-Generation X in 1998 was integral to The Rock's burgeoning career. Not only did it pit the faction he led against the most notorious stable in WWE history, it ignited his career-long battle with DX founder Triple H. Following *WrestleMania XIV*, The Rock and Triple H embarked on parallel paths. Each assumed control over a group of Superstars while proving his mettle as a title holder: Triple H as the European Champion, and The Rock as the Intercontinental Champion. For the next two decades, their careers continued to mirror each other. Each rose to main event status, became a household name, and ultimately achieved further success outside of the ring.

In 1998, D-Generation X was white hot. This rebellious group had just become fan-favorites and set the sports-entertainment world on fire by raiding a live broadcast of WWE's competitor, World Championship Wrestling. Enter The Nation of Domination, who sparked a brawl with the faction by inserting themselves into fellow Nation member Owen Hart's European Championship Match against Triple H, causing DX to retaliate. This was the first, but far from the last, time these two groups had to be separated by WWE officials. A series of heated contests set the stage for WWE's *King of the Ring* tournament. Triple H was WWE's reigning *King of the Ring*, having won the 1997 edition of the 16-man tournament. That year, he was ousted in the second round by The Rock, who went all the way to the tournament finals, before losing to Ken Shamrock.

D-Generation X attacks The Rock during his *King of the Ring* qualifying Match against Triple H (*RAW*, June 16, 1998).

"The Crock just came from the bathroom and pheeew! You should have smelled what The Rock was cookin'!"

Triple H

Ramping up the rivalry

The following night, an infuriated DX attacked The Rock. The ensuing slugfest spilled into the backstage area. While the rivalry between the two sides escalated physically, the war of words was equally brutal. On a July episode of *RAW*, DX showed that imitation was not always the sincerest form of flattery. They performed a biting impersonation of their chief rivals, referring to the Nation leader as "The Crock." The Nation was enraged, and gained a measure of revenge later that month when The Rock dealt out a Rock Bottom to Triple H, allowing D-Lo Brown to pin him for the European Championship.

"Triple H, The Rock is really flattered but there is nobody, and The Rock means NOBODY, that could ever be The People's Champ, jabroni!"

The Rock reacting to DX's impersonation

D-Generation X's Road Dogg gets the People's Elbow during a Street Fight against The Nation (*RAW*, August 17, 1998).

The Rock and Triple H battle to a draw in a 2-out-of-3 Falls Match (*In Your House: Fully Loaded*, June 26, 1998).

Street-fighting men

The Rock led his squad into the *In Your House: Fully Loaded* event prepared to defend his Intercontinental Championship in a 2-out-of-3 Falls Match against Triple H. After interference from several parties, the match ended in a time-limit draw, allowing the defending champ to hold onto his title.

Over a controversial and contentious summer, one fact became clear: When the The Nation met D-Generation X, law and order went out the window. Realizing this, WWE management scheduled a Street Fight. In a Street Fight, rules are nonexistent, and on the August 17 episode of *RAW*, both sides took advantage. Commentator Jerry Lawler wondered which hardware store each team stopped at before the bout as the ring was strewn with a myriad of household items. In a contest that scarcely resembled a wrestling match, combatants blasted each other with any metal object within reach. The match was so out of hand, no winner was declared, but seeing Triple H lying motionless from a collision with a ladder was a victory by Nation standards.

Ladder fury

At *SummerSlam 1998*, ladders were once again brought to the fore as the two faction leaders competed in a Ladder Match. In what would prove to be the final showdown between the two clans, the first Superstar to climb the ladder and retrieve the dangling International Title would become the new champion. The Rock knew that Triple H was carrying a knee injury and exploited this weakness. He later inflicted further agony by reversing a Pedigree attempt into a Back Body Drop move, so that Triple H landed flat on top of a ladder. Mark Henry attempted to intervene, but was thwarted by the DX enforcer Chyna. Triple H then evened the odds by wielding a chair.

The race to the top

The Rock eventually draped Triple H on top of a ladder and followed up by dropping a punishing People's Elbow on his prostrate rival. Normally, this would spell the end for an opponent, but Triple H is no ordinary opponent and a Ladder Match is no ordinary match. Triple H recovered just in time to interrupt The Rock's slow, exhausted climb to the ladder's top rung. With both men struggling to find sufficient energy to climb, Mark Henry made his presence felt by tossing flour into Triple H's eyes. Chyna, however, countered Henry's devious ploy by blasting The Rock with a low blow. This allowed the temporarily blinded Triple H to feel his way to the ladder's apex and seize the Intercontinental Title.

Triple H's win over The Rock was a decisive blow to The Nation. It meant Triple H and his team had seized the Intercontinental Championship from the Nation, effectively ending the rivalry between the two stables. The defeat was difficult for The Great One to take. However, The Rock would not be without championship gold for long.

Triple H crashes down on The Rock in a Ladder Match (*SummerSlam*, August 30, 1998).

THE CORPORATE CHAMPION

THE ROCK was sports entertainment's fastest rising star, a far cry from the Rocky Maivia character who had been booed out of arenas. His career was less than two years old, but he was already on an incredible journey. It seemed certain that the charismatic star would capture the WWE Championship and become one of the most popular heroes in WWE history. Then the unthinkable happened: The newly crowned People's Champion suddenly went corporate.

"The Rock never sold out. The Rock just got ahead."

The Rock

Vince and Shane McMahon are amused as the new Corporate Champion The Rock boasts of his allegiance to them (*RAW*, November 16, 1998).

The Rock's hold over the WWE Universe had become so powerful that The Nation of Domination group had disbanded with little fanfare. A single, unmistakable voice now reverberated off the rafters, commanding the enthralled crowd to "smell what he was cookin'." Now solo, The Rock was eager to back up his People's Champion moniker by seizing the WWE Championship. Standing in his way was a corporate tyrant, WWE Chairman Mr. McMahon.

The Chairman used The Rock's popularity against him to punish the WWE Universe and exert his clout as ruler of WWE's governing stable, The Corporation. Calling The Rock "The People's Chump" and "The People's Ass," McMahon continually stacked the odds against him and sought to drive him from WWE. With a tournament looming at *Survivor Series 1998* for the vacant WWE Championship, The Rock remained defiant.

"The Rock says, he would much rather be the People's Ass than to ever kiss yours," he proclaimed. In the early rounds of the tournament, The Rock ousted McMahon enforcer Big Bossman and then his *WrestleMania XIV* opponent, Ken Shamrock. With just one victory needed to reach the finals, he received a timely assist from Kane, whose involvement led to a disqualification win over Undertaker.

As Stone Cold lay beaten, Rock adds insult to injury by filming the scene himself (*Backlash*, April 25, 1999).

The Rock celebrates his win against Mankind with the McMahons (*Survivor Series*, November 15, 1998).

Facing Mankind in the finals, The Rock claimed his first WWE Championship with a victory by submission. This should have sent fans into a joyous frenzy. Instead, the manner of The Rock's victory left fans shocked and disheartened. As he locked Mankind in his Sharpshooter hold, Mr. McMahon ordered that the bell be rung, ending the match, even though Mankind had not tapped out. (The Chairman had used the same underhand tactic the previous year to snatch the title away from Bret Hart in favor of Shawn Michaels, in what became known as the Montreal Screwjob.)

The following night, The Rock was introduced as "The Corporate Champion." Explaining why he had chosen the deep pockets of WWE's big cheese at the expense of his blue-collar followers, he reminded the angry crowd of the derisive chants they had hurled at him during his rookie year: "Will some of you call The Rock a kiss-ass? I'm sure you will," he explained. "Because you are all unintelligent pieces of trailer park trash!"

The Rock subsequently abandoned any association with "the people," renaming his signature move The Corporate Elbow and his famous facial expression The Corporate Eyebrow. With his new company perks, the McMahons' new "crown jewel" seemed content to do their bidding.

While hobnobbing with the establishment, The Rock sparked two of his most epic rivalries. First, Mankind came for the WWE Championship with a vengeance. As 1998 gave way to 1999, the title bounced like a volleyball between the two Superstars. Then, The Rock and his suited cronies found themselves targeted by the antithesis of corporate snobbery, Stone Cold Steve Austin. After dousing The Corporation in beer, Stone Cold went on to defeat The Rock at *WrestleMania XV*. After he failed to regain the title weeks later at *Backlash*, The Rock blamed the loss on Mr. McMahon's son Shane, whose attempt to interfere on his behalf had backfired. Biting insults were exchanged, prompting Shane to fire The Rock and order his cronies to attack him.

After his unceremonious split from the McMahons' power-hungry faction, the WWE Universe was eager to forgive The Rock. Soon after, the reminted People's Champion once again rose to the top of the heap.

To the fans' delight, The Rock tells off The Corporation and breaks from the stable (*RAW*, April 26, 1999).

RIVALRIES
MANKIND

THE NICKNAME "Mrs. Foley's Baby Boy" might not have the same gravitas as "The Great One," but Mick Foley gave The Rock all he could handle. Assuming his most deranged persona as a masked outcast called Mankind, Foley made The Corporate Champion earn every thread of the $500 shirts he boasted about wearing. Over a three-month period beginning in November of 1998, The Rock and Foley battled each other five times for the WWE Championship, raising the level of chaos with each brutal encounter.

Mankind applies his dreaded Mandible Claw hold to *The Rock (In Your House: Rock Bottom,* December 13, 1998).

"When you can't take anymore, you will look up at me with that ridiculous eyebrow and you will say those two magic words— I quit! I quit! I quit!"

Mankind

Prior to *Survivor Series 1998*, The Rock had had few run-ins with Mankind or the other two "Faces of Foley" —the hardscrabble Cactus Jack and mellow hippie Dude Love. The Rock met Mankind in the finals of a WWE Championship tournament, where it was revealed that Mr. McMahon was grooming him, not Mankind, to lead his company. The Chairman called for an early bell, awarding The Rock an undeserved victory. He then named WWE's upcoming pay-per-view *Rock Bottom* in honor of his new champion.

Mankind nearly spoiled *Rock Bottom* for The Rock. He seemed to be on the brink of winning the WWE Championship rematch several times, but, at the crucial moment, Mr. McMahon used his influence to prevent a fair fight. The rest of The Corporation stable were all there to do the boss's bidding at Mankind's expense. However, during a No Disqualification Match on the first *RAW* of 1999, The Rock's old rivals from D-Generation X showed up to neutralize the Chairman's corporate goons. While the two factions brawled at ringside, Stone Cold Steve Austin suddenly appeared and leveled The Rock with a chair, thus enabling Mankind to win the WWE Championship for the fist time.

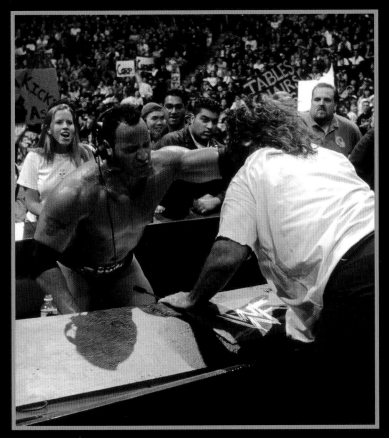

The Rock delivers amusing commentary while roughing up Mankind (*In Your House: Rock Bottom*, December 13, 1998).

The Rock insisted on a rematch: "Mankind, the least your unworthy ass can do is give The Rock a shot at what is rightfully his, and that is a shot at his WWE Title." At first, Mankind refused, but a sudden flash of inspiration changed his mind. He would grant The Rock a rematch on one condition: That it must be an "I Quit" Match.

"How does it feel, Rock," asked Mankind, "to be in a match that you can't win and I can't lose?" Notorious for his extreme tolerance for pain, Mankind had endured considerable punishment throughout his career. He had been thrown off a 20-foot cage, been entangled in barbed wire, and even lost an ear in the ring, but had never quit. If anything, pain seemed to make him smile. To regain the Championship at *Royal Rumble 1999*, The Rock would somehow have to coax this seemingly unbreakable Superstar to utter the words "I Quit."

The Rock debases Mankind in their match for the WWE Championship (*Royal Rumble*, January 24, 1999).

A winner never quits

If fans were expecting strategic holds and counter maneuvers, they were going to be disappointed. The "I Quit" Match resembled a prison fight more than a match. About two minutes after the bell, the action spilled outside the ring. Both men urged the other to quit as they wailed on each other with any blunt object light enough to lift. Mankind tumbled off a rail and crashed into a mound of equipment, causing an electrical circuit to explode. With the lights darkened, The Rock handcuffed his helpless opponent and pummeled him until he was face down on the ramp. This was the opportunity he had been waiting for.

their hatred of each other to a new level in a Last Man Standing Match. The only way to win this sort of match is to weaken your opponent so severely he is unable to stand after a ten count. Of course, no one considered what would happen if both Superstars stayed down for the count. Feeling the effects of their 22-minute slugfest, both Champion and challenger were flat out on the canvas as the referee raised his hands for the tenth time. If this rivalry was going to be settled, it would have to be in a Ladder Match.

During a brutal "I Quit" Match, The Rock demands that Mankind say the words "I Quit" (*Royal Rumble*, January 24, 1999).

Days before, Mankind had conducted an interview during which he had issued a stern promise. "You will say those two magic words—I quit! I quit! I quit!" Now, with Mankind's face hidden, a recording of his voice bellowing "I quit" played over the arena's loudspeakers, completely fooling the referee. The Rock was awarded his second WWE Championship, once again using deceitful tactics to thwart his rival.

Mankind's move

Twice robbed of the WWE Championship, Mankind pulled off a little thievery of his own. He stole a briefcase filled with $100,000.00 of The Rock's money and refused to give it back unless The Rock agreed to an Empty Arena Match, a match with no spectators. Accustomed to gloomy boiler rooms—the Boiler Room Brawl was his specialty match— Mankind thrived on silence, without the usual thousands of screaming fans in attendance. In the backstage area, Mankind proceeded to win the title back, employing one of the most resourceful moves in WWE history: He used a forklift truck to pin The Rock's shoulders to the concrete!

With *WrestleMania* just a few months away, only one man could defend the title on WWE's grandest stage. Both Mankind and The Rock were determined to be that man. On Valentine's Day, when most people celebrate love, the two rivals took

Mankind demands a rematch from The Rock in return for his stolen briefcase (*RAW*, January 25, 1999).

A sour taste

Just 24 short hours later, the two adversaries were attempting to climb a 15-foot ladder to seize the WWE Title. Watching from ringside was Stone Cold Steve Austin, who would challenge the winner at *WrestleMania*. Stone Cold did not care who won, but The Corporation did. As Mankind stood on the top rung of the ladder and stuffed his Mr. Socko puppet down The Rock's gullet, Mr. McMahon's massive new enforcer, Paul Wight (later known as Big Show), appeared on the scene and Chokeslammed Mankind to the canvas. For the third time, The Rock had won the WWE Title under dubious circumstances. The Rock may have just swallowed a gym sock, but it was Mankind leaving the building with a sour taste in his mouth.

Mankind gains the upper hand in a hard-hitting WWE Championship Match (*St. Valentine's Day Massacre*, February 14, 1999).

Mankind and The Rock battle in a Ladder Match for the WWE Championship (*RAW*, February 15, 1999).

"I've been blown up. I've been wrapped in barbed wire. I've been thrown on tacks and beds of nails. Pain is my middle name!"

Mankind

ALLIES
MANKIND

IN THE TUMULTUOUS world of WWE, Superstars often make surprising alliances—even with those with whom they have had long-running rivalries. Months after Mankind and The Rock tore each other to pieces over the WWE Championship, they ended up teaming together. Although the partnership was awkward at first, this odd couple found enough commonality to become one of the best-loved and most successful tag teams of the time.

"If ya smeeeeeelllll what The Rock... (and Sock!)... is cookin'!"

The Rock (and Mankind)

Mankind unveils the "Mr. Rocko" sock puppet (*RAW*, September 26, 1999).

"This is big, Rock.
This is important.
As a matter of fact,
This Is Your Life!"

Mankind

F acing Stone Cold Steve Austin at *WrestleMania XV*, The Rock put his vendetta with Mankind on hold. Soon after, he became fed up with toeing the line and left the McMahons' evil Corporation faction. A man of the people once again, he battled a litany of Superstars from Triple H to Mr. Ass. Months had passed since he and Mankind had bashed each other to near oblivion. The People's Champ was set to take on Big Show and Undertaker by himself when the familiar sound of screeching tires—the intro to Mankind's entrance music—filled the arena.

Mankind offered to bury the hatchet for one night only and The Rock reluctantly agreed. Despite being opposites in temperament, the two former enemies created an odd chemistry in the ring and miraculously won the World Tag Team Championships! The newly formed team was dubbed The Rock 'n' Sock Connection—a reference to Mankind's trusty puppet, Mr. Socko. Over the next several weeks, the team slowly worked to overcome their issues with each other, resulting in some of the most entertaining segments in WWE history.

As the ultimate gesture of friendship, Mankind celebrates his new ally by producing a tribute to his entire life (*RAW*, September 26, 1999).

This Is Your Life

Their most memorable segment, titled "This Is Your Life," saw Mankind host a celebration of The Great One. Complete with confetti, balloons, and even a clown named Yurple, who sang "Happy Birthday," these over-the-top festivities delighted the WWE Universe, even if they annoyed the guest of honor. One-by-one, Mankind brought people from The Rock's past to the ring, only for The Rock to greet them with a string of blistering one-liners. His sixth-grade Home Economics teacher, his high school coach, and even his high school sweetheart were dismissed as quickly as they came, receiving long-overdue putdowns for slights against The Rock. Undeterred, Mankind presented his partner with a matching Rock 'n' Sock Connection jacket, along with a sock puppet of his own named "Mr. Rocko." Though this was one of the longer segments, "This Is Your Life" became one of the most popular segments in WWE history.

A double People's Elbow to Big Show leads to a Tag Team Championship victory for The Rock and Mankind (*RAW*, August 30, 1999).

Rock 'n' Sock rule

The Rock's new ally may have irritated him with his unpredictable shenanigans and habit of stealing The Rock's catchphrases, but there was no denying that two could lay the smackdown better than one. Together they won the World Tag Team Championships three times. Their third title reign would have lasted longer, if not for a misunderstanding. Mankind showed up at *RAW* with yet another gift for his partner: an autographed copy of his new book, *Have a Nice Day!* When the book was later found in the trash, Mankind went ballistic and disowned The Rock, refusing to tag in to their title match against the Holly cousins and costing them the match. It was soon revealed that Al Snow, not The Rock, was the real culprit behind the discarded book.

> **"I give you a present, I give you something I've worked hard on, and you just throw it away?"**
>
> **Mankind, believing that The Rock had thrown his book into the trash**

The Rock 'n' Sock Connection never won the tag team title again but they did patch up their differences. They made life miserable for Triple H and Stephanie McMahon, who had assumed control over WWE as The McMahon-Helmsley faction. Aiming to split up the two troublemakers, Triple H arranged a Pink Slip On a Pole Match between them where the loser would be fired. The Rock won, but before his ally could receive his walking papers, The Rock masterminded a revolt. The entire WWE roster threatened to walk out if Mankind was not reinstated. This power play led to both men being part of the Fatal Four Way Main Event at *WrestleMania 2000*.

Over the years, The Rock has maintained a special bond with Mick Foley. On special occasions, they have reprised their partnership, most notably to battle Evolution at *WrestleMania XX*. Though they teamed for less than a year, they remain one of the most memorable pairings in WWE history—proof that anything is possible in WWE, even a handsome, sharply dressed corporate figurehead bonding with a deranged, bedraggled "lunatic."

The Rock leads the way in a Dark Side Rules Match, teaming with Mankind against Viscera and Mideon (*RAW*, September 20, 1999).

The Rock 'n' Sock Connection beats the New Age Outlaws for their third World Tag Team Championship (*SmackDown*, October 14, 1999).

THE ROCK VS. MANKIND

EMPTY ARENA MATCH DURING HALFTIME HEAT 1/31/99

While the NFL's Super Bowl game paused for halftime, WWE seized the spotlight. The Rock defended the WWE Championship in a match where the only people present were The Rock, the WWE crew, and his kooky opponent, Mankind. Because the match had no rules, The Rock was forced to compete with the same savagery as his challenger. Cameras were placed all over the arena, the backstage area, and even the parking lots to capture the chaos.

The Rock kicks Mankind around on the empty arena floor during a brutal battle.

1: EAT THIS

Mankind tries to silence The Rock's trash-talk early by shoving his trusty Mr. Socko puppet into his mouth. On commentary, Mr. McMahon bemoans the barbaric move. Mankind then rams McMahon's The Rock into the timekeeper's bell, causing a "DING" noise to echo throughout the vacant building.

2: LAYING THE TRASH DOWN

The Rock whips Mankind through the barricade and into the seats, causing an avalanche of folding chairs. He then rolls Mankind like a giant Slinky down a flight of stairs and covers him with trash, while mixing in some resounding strikes with a steel trash can.

3: NOT WHAT THE ROCK WAS COOKIN'

Crashing over pots and pans, the brawlers leave the kitchen in ruins with shattered plates and assorted items strewn about the floor. They proceed to demolish a catering table, hurling dinner trays and dousing each other with sauces and condiments. During the melee, The Rock comically complains that the hot sauce is too mild.

4: DESK DUTY

Backstage office workers flee as the two disheveled combatants burst through the door. When the desk phone rings, The Rock politely answers with, "SmackDown Hotel... Mankind is a little busy right now. His mouth is full of The Rock's foot!"

5: ROCK, PAPER... FORKLIFT?

In the loading dock area, Mankind weakens The Rock with his Mandible Claw. The deranged challenger then commandeers a forklift and pins The Rock under the weight of the machine, winning the WWE Title in controversial fashion.

THE ROCK'S ICONIC ENTRANCES

FEW ENTERTAINERS ENTER a building with as much pizzazz as The Rock. In the pantheon of crowd-pleasing Superstar ring entrances, his ranks among the most audience rousing. Just by stepping through the curtain to the sound of his unmistakable theme, The Great One raises the decibel level of the WWE Universe to ear-popping levels.

The Rock strolls down the ramp to address a sea of adoring fans (*RAW*, February 4, 2002).

The Rock strikes his signature pose on the second turnbuckle, showing off the WWE Championship (*Old School RAW*, March 4, 2013).

Rallying cries

The Rock often shouts out, "If ya smell what The Rock is cookin'!" as the finale to his WWE appearances, creating a neat bookend effect, as the same battle cry opens his entrance music. His booming voice jolts the WWE Universe to life. The pounding sound that follows has evolved over the years, but its basic rhythm has remained constant. By tweaking certain riffs and enhancing different instruments, the mood of the track reflects whatever emotions The Rock wishes to communicate, from his villainous time in The Nation through his rise to superstardom. Since his return to WWE in 2011, his signature sound has conveyed the vibe of a conquering hero returning home.

From its iconic opening salvo to its face-melting guitar squeal, The Rock's theme music is as recognizable as he is. Composed by WWE's own musical maestro, Jim Johnston—the creator of themes for Undertaker, Stone Cold Steve Austin, The Ultimate Warrior and a slew of others—its sound brilliantly captures the visceral excitement and energy that The Rock generates. Speaking to *Newsweek* in 2018, Johnston, while giving credit to The Rock for the track's popularity, offers some insightful commentary on why it fits The Great One's persona. "It defies a genre. It's not a rock song, it's not orchestral, it's not world music, it's not urban," says Johnston. "There's an element to Rock that he's a mix of a bunch of different vibes and cultures, and I thought that was an interesting, fortuitous, utterly unplanned but happy accident." While difficult to label, the name of the tune, "Electrifying," is all the classification it needs.

Posing and profiling

When entering the arena, before he even utters a word, The Rock owns the room. Bounding across the stage, he takes in his surroundings, making eye contact with the people and lapping up the applause. Strolling down the ramp, he is in no hurry to get to the ring, and often stops to interact with the fans lucky enough to be seated along the barrier. His slow and steady stroll not only builds up tension, it can also serve to psych out his nervous opponent. Before entering the ring, The Rock stands on the middle rope and thrusts his right arm into the air, his gaze sweeping around the auditorium. He then strikes the same signature pose in the opposite corner, giving spectators in all sections a golden photo opportunity.

The Rock delighted the *WrestleMania 32* crowd with a fiery entrance (April 3, 2016).

The Rock ignites the record-breaking crowd of 101,763 fans at AT&T Stadium in Arlington, Texas (*WrestleMania 32* April 3, 2016).

ROYAL RUMBLE MATCH

ROYAL RUMBLE 1/23/00

There are many roads to *WrestleMania*, but none as direct as the Royal Rumble Match. The winner of this 30-Superstar melee earns the right to challenge the WWE Champion at the Show of Shows. The 2000 edition saw The Rock go the distance for the only time in his career. Weeks before, The People's Champ boldly guaranteed that he would outlast his 29 fellow competitors, including the 500-pound Big Show. With a target on his back, the fan-favorite stood tall against the odds, but his win was not without controversy.

Crash Holly, The Rock, Val Venis, and Hardcore Holly battle in front of a raucous New York City crowd.

1: JUMPING INTO THE ACTION

After nearly 40 minutes, the WWE Universe erupts when The People's Champ emerges as the 24th entrant into the match. After all that waiting, he is spoiling for a fight. He goes after the first man he sees—Big Bossman— and eliminates him within seconds.

2: TWO ON ONE

Superstars are eager to make The Rock eat his words. He fights off several double-teams and eliminates Crash Holly, Al Snow, and X-Pac, or so he thinks. Seeing the referee is distracted, X-Pac rejoins the match as if nothing had happened!

3: FACING THE GIANT

Big Show tosses X-Pac out for good. As the giant turns around, The Rock pounces, knowing he only has one more Superstar to beat. Then he delights the New York City crowd with a Big Apple-sized People's Elbow.

4: HANGING ON

Big Show turns the tables with a thundering Chokeslam, then hoists The Rock onto his shoulders. Heading for a painful demise, The Rock desperately grabs the ring ropes and clings on for dear life as The Giant spills over the top, crashing onto the floor below.

5: VICTORIOUS

Using every ounce of his strength, The Rock avoids tumbling to the floor with his opponent, winning the match. Although a video later shows that his feet probably grazed the floor, it does not matter. He is going to *WrestleMania* and the WWE Universe is ecstatic.

CROWD PLEASERS

BEING THE PEOPLE'S Champion means always keeping one's finger on the people's pulse. The Rock has always been a master at working an audience, telling them exactly what they want to hear with the right amount of his trademark flair. With impeccable timing, a dangerous wit and an unfiltered sense of humor, his crowd-pleasing microphone work is music to the ears of everyone but his opponents.

"There is someone who The Rock considers a nothing, a nobody, a peon, a blemish on The Rock's buttocks, and this jabroni's name—and that is correct, it doesn't matter what his name is—but for the record, his name is the Road Dogg."

The Rock prepares to issue a challenge, *RAW*, November 1, 1999

"You have never impressed The Rock. From the time your crappy music hits,'Weelllll it's the Big Slooooww!' And every single Rock fan stops, pauses and says this, 'I'm going to go take a leak. This guy sucks!'"

The Rock to Big Show, *RAW*, August 9, 1999

"On one hand, you've got a man who revolutionized the industry, a man who appeals to all generations and truth be told, the biggest star the industry has ever and will ever see. And on the other hand you've got...Hulk Hogan."

The Rock insults Hulk Hogan on
***SmackDown*, January 30, 2003**

"Jericho's claim to be the best, The Rock has found quite brutal. Clearly, Chris Jericho is a man who has no strudel. 'I am a living legend,' Y2J would sing As he trembled with fear heading into the people's ring. And faster, faster than Scrooge saw the Ghost of Christmas Past The Rock hit the people's ring and whipped Y2J's ass!"

The Rock with some holiday poetry,
***RAW* December 24, 2001**

"All the stars came out. You've got The Rock, Busta Rhymes, and Doctor Evil himself, right here."

The Rock likens Kurt Angle to Austin Powers' nemesis,
***SmackDown* July 11, 2002**

"The Rock can just imagine you in high school, the oldest 27 year old senior the world has ever seen. The teacher says 'OK class, what is two plus two? Do you know, Booker?' 'Oh yeah, I know the answer to that... Thomas Jefferson, sucka!'"

The Rock imagines Booker T's high school days on *RAW*, August 13, 2001

"...Drink some Steveweisers, listen to some Backstreet Boys..."

The Rock roasts all five of his Armageddon opponents, finishing off with a jab at Stone Cold's taste in music. *RAW*, December 4, 1999

"'Oh dear God, my name is Billy. I just won King of the Ring, but there is one problem, everybody still thinks that I absolutely suck!' And then your house started to shake, the heavens opened up and God said this, 'Bob?' 'But my name is Billy...' 'It doesn't matter what your name is!'"

The Rock's rendition of Billy Gunn's prayers to God on *HEAT*, July 11, 1999

"Chris Jericho, I can't believe you are still talking about the night you beat Stone Cold Steve Austin and myself! I guess it is better than talking about the haircut that makes you look like a twelve-year-old boy."

The Rock calls out his old rival, Jericho, for his loud, spikey haircut. *WWE Hall of Fame Induction Ceremony*, **March 29, 2008**

"Did The Rock hurt your feelings? You wipe your 400-pound ass with your feelings!"

After Rikishi costs him the WWE Title, The Rock has zero sympathy for his feelings, *RAW*, **October 23, 2000**

"Well I might take a plane,
I might take a train,
How do you people live here,
You must be insane.

I'm leaving Sacramento,
Sacramento I won't stay;
But I'll be sure to come back when
the Lakers beat the Kings in May."

**The Rock insults the hometown basketball
team in a song called "Leaving Sacramento"
RAW, Sacramento, California, March 24, 2003**

The first Rock Concert.
(*RAW*, Sacramento, California,
March 24, 2003)

"Warden threw a party and he spent some bucks,
Didn't invite Cena 'cause he totally sucks.
Cena started rapping, it all went south,
Know your role Jabroni and shut your mouth.
Let's rock! Everybody let's rock!
Cena's got a menstrual clock,
But we're dancing 'cause Cleveland Rocks!"

Insults turn personal as The Rock sings about John Cena while spoofing Elvis Presley's "*Jailhouse Rock.*" *RAW*, March 12, 2012

"You ain't nothin' but a redneck,
Crying all the time.
You ain't nothin' but a redneck,
Crying all the time.
Well you ain't gonna beat The Rock.
Your candy ass is mine!"

The Rock sings about Stone Cold Steve Austin, to the tune of "You Ain't Nuthin' But a Hound Dog." Austin then bursts in, knocks The Rock out of the ring, grabs his guitar (that has been signed by country music legend Willie Nelson) and destroys it. *RAW, Sacramento, California, March 24, 2003*

THE ATTITUDE ERA

WWE HAS ALWAYS evolved to give its passionate fans the entertainment they crave. During the late 1990s, the WWE Universe wanted a grittier, edgier show, with more realistic Superstars and adult themes. WWE was also being challenged by a rival, World Championship Wrestling (WCW), whose Monday Nitro program had taken many viewers away from WWE's flagship show, *Monday Night RAW*. To survive, WWE not only had to adapt to changing times, it also needed to invent ways to capture higher ratings than WCW. The result was the birth of The Attitude Era, an infamous five-year period when anything could and did happen in WWE, thanks to the rise of intrepid Superstars such as Stone Cold Steve Austin, D-Generation X, Mankind, and, of course, The Rock.

Facing chief rival Mankind, The Rock wins with swagger, counting the three-count with his free hand (*RAW*, December 14, 1998).

The Rock is full of attitude as he glares at Triple H (*SmackDown*, August 24, 1999).

r. McMahon warned viewers that changes were in store, advising that some of the action might be too strong or scandalous for some people. He promised that RAW would prove to be "The Cure for the Common Show" and delivered on his promise. Gone were the days of heroes telling fans to "say their prayers and take their vitamins" and cartoonish characters such as Doink the Clown. In their place were rebellious antiheroes who drank beer, insulted the boss, and shocked fans each week with increasingly irreverent and inventive antics.

Even Mr. McMahon got into the act. For years, his status as the head honcho of WWE had never been mentioned. After a controversy at *Survivor Series 1997*, in which he cheated Bret Hart out of the WWE Title, fans became acutely aware that he was in charge. Realizing his past treatment of Hart had made him unpopular, the Chairman evolved into an evil, domineering authority figure, one of The Attitude Era's most ruthless villains. When Stone Cold Steve Austin defied him, he fulfilled the dreams of millions of blue-collar workers who fantasized about doing the same thing to their bosses. As Austin led the charge against the powers that be, a faction named D-Generation X infuriated censors by bringing juvenile humor to the ring. The Rock fit in perfectly, pushing boundaries each time he picked up a microphone. The more outrageous he and his peers became, the louder the WWE Universe roared with approval.

D-Generation X entertains the crowd with their sophomoric brand of humor (*RAW*, January 19, 1998).

Stone Cold Steve Austin floors the WWE Chairman, Mr. McMahon, with a Stunner (*RAW*, June 1, 1998).

College-aged people flocked to shows, filling arenas with homemade signs and chants that mirrored the fearless creativity of the Superstars. Amidst all the fun and revelry, in-ring competition became more intense. Matches were hard-hitting affairs, and more extreme elements such as tables, thumbtacks, and other everyday weapons were more commonplace than they are today. During this time, many famous match-types were invented that over the years have altered careers and produced jaw-dropping highlights.

Kane is set ablaze by his brother Undertaker in an Inferno Match (*Unforgiven*, April 26, 1998).

Edge and Christian, The Hardy Boyz, and The Dudley Boyz made the Tables, Ladders, and Chairs match a part of WWE lore. These three teams revolutionized tag team wrestling by plummeting from ladders and performing other high-risk stunts. Hell in a Cell was also invented, leading Undertaker to hurl Mankind from the cage's 20-foot-high roof through the announcers' table. Undertaker's disturbing half-brother Kane emerged, initiating a series of gruesome contests that included the First Blood Match, where the loser is the first to bleed, and the Inferno Match, in which the loser is the first to be set on fire.

A good attitude

The Rock spent the bulk of his WWE career as part of The Attitude Era. Competing during this time gave him the freedom to unleash his true personality. Although his drive and talent would have seen him succeed in any era, he was particularly suited to this period. His frequent references to his opponent's "candy ass" would not have been allowed in more family friendly times, to say nothing of some of his other insults. Undoubtedly, The Great One still would have cooked up some entertaining one-liners, but acheiving the same shock factor would have been a tall task.

The Attitude Era ended during the period that The Rock was preparing to leap into acting full-time. Unlike its beginning, there was no formal address from Mr. McMahon announcing its end. Once the Superstars responsible for bringing the attitude departed, it just fizzled out, replaced by a new era of competitors and a new elixir of excitement called "Ruthless Aggression." WWE will likely never revert to the unfiltered debauchery that defined the late 1990s and early 2000s. Instead, The Attitude Era lives in the WWE annals as a "perfect storm," in which the right people came together at the right time.

Undertaker hurls Mankind through the roof of Hell in a Cell (*King of the Ring*, June 28, 1998).

The Attitude Era's influence is still felt throughout sports entertainment. The Rock, Stone Cold, and their peers proved that a Superstar did not need some cartoony persona to entertain the WWE Universe. They simply channeled their real-life personalities, as if someone had hooked them up to an amplifier and turned the dial up to eleven. Modern day standouts, such as John Cena, The Miz, Sasha Banks, and The New Day might not be as scandalous, but they have achieved great success by applying the same formula. Future generations of Superstars will surely take note, and the success stories of this turbulent time are sure to embolden others to take chances, embrace controversy, and unleash their true selves.

WWE's Attitude Era DVD cover from 2012 featured many of the era's top stars.

RIVALRIES
STONE COLD STEVE AUSTIN

MATCHES HEADLINED "The Rock vs. Stone Cold Steve Austin" were must-see events—fans could not get enough. After a rousing *WrestleMania XV* main event, the two Superstars headlined *WrestleMania X-Seven* two years later. They then clashed a third time at *WrestleMania XIX*. The Rock and Austin then became the first Superstars to face each other three times on WWE's Grandest Stage—twice in the main event. These two strong personalities epitomized The Attitude Era, and their rivalry lives on in WWE lore as one of the greatest of all time.

> "You can walk your little carcass out here and raise your eyebrow up as many times as you want!"
>
> **Stone Cold Steve Austin**

Stone Cold Steve Austin unleashes his signature Stunner move on The Rock (*RAW*, December 20, 1998).

tone Cold Steve Austin was a bad-tempered Texan who set the tone for a meaner, grittier WWE with his blue-collar toughness and foul-mouthed aggression. Austin's path of destruction had already begun when Rocky Maivia debuted in late 1996. He crossed paths with Maivia a year later, when Maivia had developed a new persona, and Stone Cold was defending the Intercontinental Championship. Their brief clash was just a preview of what was to come. Rather than relinquish the Intercontinental Title to The Rock, as he was ordered to, Austin hurled the belt into a New England river. For the rest of their careers, the two rivals competed with the same unrelenting defiance, regardless of the stakes.

A new rival

The first clash over the WWE Championship at *WrestleMania XV* belonged to Austin, but The Rock's revenge was as harsh as it was symbolic. He lured Austin to a nearby river, echoing Austin's previous stunt. The Rock not only tossed the WWE Title into the water but sent Austin for a swim as well, throwing him off a bridge. Some weeks later, The Rock renounced his association with Austin's chief antagonists, the McMahons and The Corporation, but their mutual animosity never disappeared. As big as WWE was, it was not big enough for two Superstars of this magnitude to coexist in peace. It was inevitable that their common goals would drive them to battle each other once again.

Stone Cold Steve Austin rallies with a series of brutal strikes (*WrestleMania X-Seven*, April 1, 2001).

Stone Cold exits

After thwarting Austin's coup in the fall of 2001, The Rock turned his attention to other conquests. Yet he never forgot his two *WrestleMania* losses to his nemesis, and challenged Austin to face him one more time at *WrestleMania XIX*. This time, no titles were at stake but a third Austin win would have been devastating to The Rock's legacy. Fortunately for his millions of fans, The Great One earned the win. Stone Cold Steve Austin never competed again, leaving the WWE Universe to forever debate which of these two icons got the best of their career-long vendetta.

The Rock attempts to wear Austin down with a headlock (*WrestleMania X-Seven*, March 28, 1999).

WrestleMania X-Seven took place in Stone Cold's backyard, the Astrodome in Houston, Texas; however, Stone Cold was anything but a hometown hero. He had formed an alliance with Mr. McMahon, who had helped him defeat The Rock again for the WWE Championship. This shocking turn of events was the polar opposite of their earlier battles and added a new twist to their rivalry. Austin was now a power-hungry villain under the influence of the evil Chairman, while The Rock was a rebel against the establishment. Mr. McMahon should have known not to trust the Texas Rattlesnake. Before long, Austin had betrayed him to lead The Alliance, a faction bent on destroying WWE. The Chairman was then forced to ask The Rock to save his company from a hostile takeover.

The Rock is a man possessed in his third *WrestleMania* clash against Austin (*WrestleMania XIX*, March 30, 2003).

TIMELINE
THE ROCK VS. STONE COLD STEVE AUSTIN

EVERY ERA IN WWE history has its definitive Superstar. The Attitude Era had two: The Rock and Stone Cold Steve Austin, though neither had any desire to share his perch atop sports entertainment. These polar opposites—The Rock with his showy displays of fortune and Austin dressed as if atop a tractor—were at each other's throats for nearly six years. This bitter rivalry propelled both Superstars, and as a result, WWE, to unprecedented heights.

INTERCONTINENTAL SPLASH
RAW: Stone Cold appears on the Titantron to badmouth The Nation. To the faction's dismay, he proceeds to toss The Rock's Intercontinental Title into a river.

Dec 15, 1997

| Nov 17, 1997 | Nov 24, 1997 | Dec 7, 1997 | Dec 8, 1997 | Jan 18, 1998 |

GRAND THEFT TITLE
RAW: The Nation ambushes Stone Cold Steve Austin. Rocky Maivia seizes the chance to slip in and swipe the Intercontinental Championship belt.

BEEP 3:16
RAW: Referring to his famous "Austin 3:16" catchphrase, Stone Cold sends the numbers "3:16" to The Rock's beeper (a device that predated cell phones). The ominous message means that Austin is closing in and ready to attack!

FORFEITING AUSTIN STYLE
RAW: Refusing to defend the Intercontinental Championship on WWE Chairman Mr. McMahon's terms, Austin forfeits to The Rock. Instead of leaving the ring quietly, Austin then drops the new champ with a Stunner.

THE FIRST OF MANY
In Your House: D-Generation X: Although he had yet to win the title, The Rock proclaims himself to be "the best damn Intercontinental Champion ever." At the *In Your House: D-Generation X* event, Stone Cold silences him by winning their first-ever title match against each other and retaining the title.

FINAL TWO
Royal Rumble: The Rock and Stone Cold are the final two Superstars left standing in the 30-Man Royal Rumble Match. Stone Cold claims victory by using a Stunner to propel The Rock over the ropes.

FIRST TITLE DEFENSE

RAW: One day after winning the WWE Championship for the first time, "Corporate Champion" The Rock defends the gold against Stone Cold. "The Rattlesnake" looks to have the title won, when Undertaker arrives with a shovel and lays him out. The Rock thus retains the title.

NUMBER ONE CONTENDER

RAW: After winning the title back in a Ladder Match, The Rock is attacked by the new number one contender, Stone Cold Steve Austin.

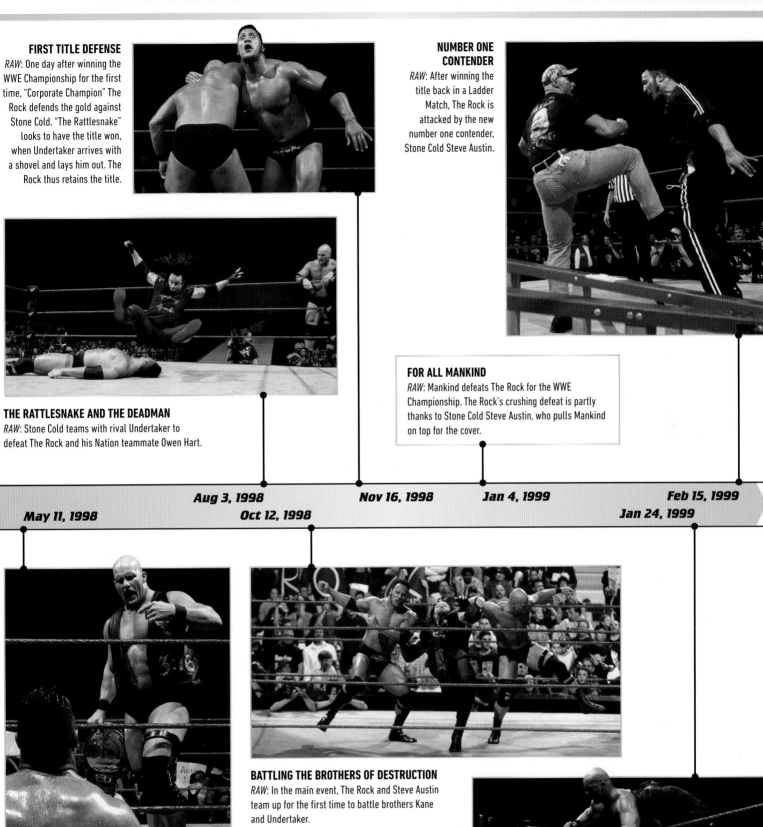

THE RATTLESNAKE AND THE DEADMAN

RAW: Stone Cold teams with rival Undertaker to defeat The Rock and his Nation teammate Owen Hart.

FOR ALL MANKIND

RAW: Mankind defeats The Rock for the WWE Championship. The Rock's crushing defeat is partly thanks to Stone Cold Steve Austin, who pulls Mankind on top for the cover.

May 11, 1998

Aug 3, 1998

Oct 12, 1998

Nov 16, 1998

Jan 4, 1999

Jan 24, 1999

Feb 15, 1999

MYSTERY PARTNER

RAW: The Rock and fellow Nation member D-Lo Brown agree to battle Austin and a mystery partner selected by Mr. McMahon. To mess with Austin, Mr. McMahon selects himself.

BATTLING THE BROTHERS OF DESTRUCTION

RAW: In the main event, The Rock and Steve Austin team up for the first time to battle brothers Kane and Undertaker.

MR. MCMAHON GOES THE DISTANCE

Royal Rumble: All Stone Cold has to do is eliminate Mr. McMahon to win the Royal Rumble Match. This seems like an easy task, until The Rock distracts him, helping the Chairman to pull off a surprise win.

TIMELINE
THE ROCK VS. STONE COLD STEVE AUSTIN

MEMORIAL MELEE
RAW: The Rock stages a "funeral" to mock his rival's demise from the previous week. Austin interrupted his own eulogy by driving a monster truck over The Rock's limousine.

BEER BATH
RAW: Stone Cold interrupts The Corporation by crashing into the arena driving a beer truck. He toasts his and The Rock's upcoming *WrestleMania* match by dousing himself and his cronies with beer.

SWING AND A MISS
No Mercy: Intending to help Austin, The Rock tries to hit their mutual enemy Triple H with a sledgehammer. He accidentally strikes Austin, costing him the match.

Mar 22, 1999		Apr 19, 1999			Oct 17, 1999
	Mar 28, 1999		Apr 12, 1999	Apr 25, 1999	Apr 29, 1999

SMOKIN' SKULL GOES FOR A SWIM
RAW: Upon becoming WWE Champion, Stone Cold demanded the return of his personalized "Smokin' Skull" title belt. Rather than simply hand it to him, The Rock threw the title and Austin into a river.

NEW SHOW, NEW PARTNERS
SmackDown: On the first-ever episode of *SmackDown*, The Rock and Austin are forced to team up. The unlikely duo battle Triple H and Undertaker to a "no contest" finish.

EPISODE ONE
WrestleMania XV: In the first chapter of their *WrestleMania* trilogy, Austin prevails, to become WWE Champion.

ONE RULE, NO RULES
Backlash: At the first-ever *Backlash* event, a rematch is held with Shane McMahon as the special guest referee. In this lawless, No Holds Barred encounter, Austin overcomes the odds to remain champion, and also takes back his "Smokin' Skull" title.

AUSTIN IS BACK

Backlash: Sidelined for months after being hit by a car driving by Rikishi, Stone Cold returns during *Backlash 2000*. Wielding a chair, he attacks the McMahons and Triple H, helping The Rock to win the WWE Championship.

TRUST ISSUES

SmackDown: The Rock insists that he had nothing to do with Rikishi's automobile assault. Stone Cold has his doubts, and gives him a Stunner. Later that night, The Rock repays him with a Rock Bottom.

IT'S ON... AGAIN

RAW: After becoming the new WWE Champion, The Rock has a tense exchange with Austin, knowing that they will square off once again for the title at *WrestleMania*.

Apr 30, 2000	Nov 2, 2000		Feb 26, 2001	
	Oct 9, 2000	Nov 9, 2000	Dec 14, 2000	Mar 12, 2001

"I DID IT FOR THE ROCK"

RAW: The Rock's cousin, Rikishi, admitted that he was the mystery assailant who ran over Stone Cold with a car. Rikishi claimed The Rock, not Austin, deserved to be the top Superstar in WWE.

THE TRUTH COMES OUT

SmackDown: After learning that Triple H is the real mastermind behind the car attack, The Rock and Austin agree to team up. However, they are blindsided by the Radicalz.

SHORT-TERM ALLIES

SmackDown: The Rock and Austin team up to defeat WWE Champion Kurt Angle and European Champion William Regal, who bring the monstrous Kane along for backup.

DOMESTIC TANGLE

RAW: Mr. McMahon forces Austin's wife, Debra, to become The Rock's manager. When Debra is injured during The Rock's match against Kurt Angle, Austin punishes The Rock by attacking him.

TIMELINE
THE ROCK VS. STONE COLD STEVE AUSTIN

LOST SHAKER OF SALT
RAW: The Rock calls out Austin, who is captaining anti-WWE faction The Alliance. The duo eases the tension between them by singing the song "Margaritaville" together. When the fun is over, The Rock flattens Austin, claiming he'll never forget what happened at *WrestleMania*.

DEFENDING WWE
Survivor Series: Representing Team WWE in a Traditional *Survivor Series* Elimination Match, The Rock earns the final pin on Team Alliance captain Stone Cold, forcing The Alliance to disband.

LESSONS IN LOYALTY
RAW: Making his first appearance on *RAW* in several months, The Rock has some harsh criticism for Stone Cold, who has recently walked out of WWE.

THE ROCK STRIKES BACK
RAW: When Austin arrives to interfere in The Rock's Handicap Match, he is dealt a Rock Bottom in retribution for the previous week.

Mar 19, 2001		Nov 12, 2001	Nov 18, 2001	Jun 17, 2002	
	Apr 01, 2001	Apr 02, 2001		Dec 06, 2001	Feb 24, 2003

WHY, AUSTIN? WHY?
RAW: Disgusted by Austin's actions, The Rock tries to reclaim the title in a Steel Cage Match. He wins by disqualification. By rule, Austin keeps the title. To make matters worse, Austin and Triple H brutally attack and injure The Rock.

MUTUAL ADMIRATION
SmackDown: World Heavyweight Champion The Rock and WWE Champion Stone Cold toast each other, believing that soon one of them will become Undisputed Champion.

HOUSTON, WE HAVE A PROBLEM
WrestleMania X-Seven: Stone Cold defeats The Rock for the WWE Championship. Unlike his win two years previously, this victory is tainted by Austin's shocking alliance with Mr. McMahon, which dismays the Houston crowd.

HOLLYWOOD EGO
RAW: The Rock berates the WWE Universe for voting Stone Cold the Superstar of the Decade. He claims Stone Cold, who has just returned, is "nothing" compared to him.

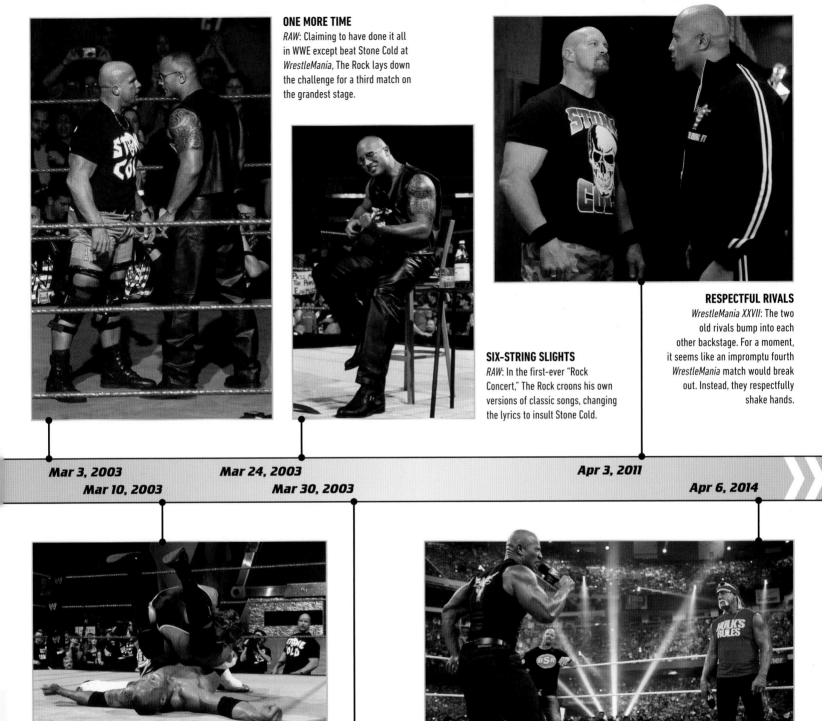

ONE MORE TIME

RAW: Claiming to have done it all in WWE except beat Stone Cold at *WrestleMania*, The Rock lays down the challenge for a third match on the grandest stage.

SIX-STRING SLIGHTS

RAW: In the first-ever "Rock Concert," The Rock croons his own versions of classic songs, changing the lyrics to insult Stone Cold.

RESPECTFUL RIVALS

WrestleMania XXVII: The two old rivals bump into each other backstage. For a moment, it seems like an impromptu fourth *WrestleMania* match would break out. Instead, they respectfully shake hands.

Mar 3, 2003

Mar 10, 2003

Mar 24, 2003

Mar 30, 2003

Apr 3, 2011

Apr 6, 2014

WHAT'S UP WITH THAT?

RAW: The Rock suffers an embarrassing defeat to lovable underdog Superstar The Hurricane, thanks to interference by Stone Cold.

THE FINAL CHAPTER

WrestleMania XIX: After an amazing three Rock Bottoms, The Rock finally pins Stone Cold at *WrestleMania*. Following the match, Austin retires from in-ring competition.

THREE AT THE MIC

WrestleMania: The Rock interrupts Austin in the opening segment of *WrestleMania XXX*, but not to give him a Rock Bottom. He joins Austin and Hulk Hogan in hyping the night's event. The three icons then share a special toast.

THE ROCK VS. STONE COLD STEVE AUSTIN
WRESTLEMANIA XIX 03/30/03

The Rock had little left to prove in WWE, but one thing still played to his ego: he had never beaten Stone Cold Steve Austin at *WrestleMania*. He had fallen to his nemesis in two previous attempts. Hoping to atone for these failures, he challenged Stone Cold to face him once again on WWE's grandest stage for a third time with high stakes. The winner of the match would own the final bragging rights in their rivalry.

The Rock and Austin stare each other down for the third and final time at *WrestleMania*.

1: SHARP TACTICS
Austin enters the match wearing knee braces to protect his damaged knees. Noticing this key weakness, The Rock attacks them as much as possible, delivering targeted strikes. Focusing on the one area where his opponent is vulnerable is a cruel, yet savvy strategy.

2: ROLE REVERSAL
With the advantage, The Rock taunts Austin by putting on Austin's trademark vest. The brazen move only infuriates Austin, who retaliates by borrowing something of The Rock's: his patented Rock Bottom maneuver.

3: OH HELL NO!

The Rock is not about to lose to his own finishing move. But neither is Austin. After The Rock returns the favor by using the Stone Cold Stunner, Austin responds by hitting his opponent with the authentic version. Unlike previous *WrestleManias*, the maneuver does not finish off The Rock.

4: TAMING THE RATTLESNAKE

After the rivals trade Stunners, The Rock goes for the People's Elbow. Austin dodged his first attempt but not the second. Smelling victory, The Rock sheds Stone Cold's vest and moves in for the decisive blow.

5: THIRD TIME'S THE CHARM

Austin kicks out of not one, but two Rock Bottoms, shocking the Seattle crowd. Like a man possessed, The Rock unleashes an amazing third Rock Bottom. This time the referee counts to three, finally ending The Rock's futility against his biggest foe.

THE HURRICANE
A CATEGORY 5 UPSET

ALL WWE SUPERSTARS are living comic book superheroes or super villains to some degree. The Hurricane just took it to new Kryptonian levels, dashing into action cloaked in an emerald skinsuit complete with a mask, cape, and H emblem on his chest. His noble quest to hold WWE's coldblooded offenders accountable for their deeds was admirable. Still, not in comic guru Stan Lee's wildest dreams would anyone consider his "Hurripowers" a threat to a Superstar of The Rock's ilk—except for those three weeks in the winter of 2003, when (aided by Stone Cold Steve Austin) The Rock suffered his most embarrassing defeat. This brief run-in delivered so much entertainment that it must be celebrated.

The Rock

Hometown: Miami, Florida

Height: 6ft 5in (1.95m)

Weight: 260lb (116kg)

*Championships: WWE (7), WCW (2), Intercontinental (2), World Tag Team (5)

Humble origin: A smiley "blue chip" recruit covered in ribbons

Catchphrase: Too many to list

WrestleMania **matches:** 6

The Hurricane

Hometown: Unknown

Height: 6ft (1.82m)

Weight: 215lb (97.52kg)

*Championships: World Tag Team (1), European (1), Hardcore (1), Cruiserweight (2)

Humble origin: A boy-band tag team called 3 Count

Catchphrase: "What's up with that?!"

WrestleMania **matches:** 2 (sort of... both were backstage for the Hardcore Title and lasted under 10 seconds)

ADVANTAGE: THE ROCK

*As of March 10, 2003

SMACK TALK:

"The Rock knows who you are. With the green shirt, 'H' on your shirt, and the mask. You're the Hamburglar from McDonalds! Go get The Rock a cheeseburger!"

The Rock dismisses The Hurricane as an affable fast food mascot

"I know one superhero who I can definitely beat, The Scorpion King!"

The Hurricane hits back hard, insulting The Rock's signature movie role at the time

ADVANTAGE: EVEN

IN THE RING: THE MIRACLE IN CLEVELAND

"Miracle" is a bit dramatic, but for a city known for sports futility it was an uplifting moment for the locals, not to mention the millions at home embittered by The Rock's recent attitude. How does an upset of this magnitude happen? In six steps:

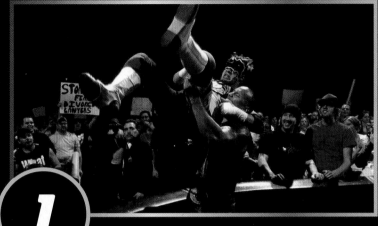

1 Normal boundaries are immediately crossed. With No Disqualification rules in effect, the stronger combatant becomes the aggressor.

2 The Rock, an over-confident villain, slaps the green-clad underdog around, then parades around in his cape. To be fair, The Rock's physique is better fit for superhero garb.

3 Real antagonists are not satisfied with just winning. They wish to demoralize their foes. Instead of going for an easy pin, The Rock inflicts more pain upon his adversary.

4 The plucky protagonist makes his assailant pay for his arrogance. He finds a second wind and goes to his greatest strength. For The Hurricane, that means a leap of faith.

5 The hero makes an intelligent play, striking a legal low blow under No Disqualification rules, softening up his competitor for a brutal Chokeslam.

6 Help arrives at the most opportune moment. The Rock's nemesis, Stone Cold Steve Austin, distracts him, allowing The Hurricane to score a shocking pin!

ADVANTAGE: THE HURRICANE (WITH PARTIAL CREDIT TO STONE COLD STEVE AUSTIN)

ATTITUDE ERA
RIVALS GALLERY

No one likes being called a jabroni, especially the fierce Superstars who ruled WWE alongside The Rock during The Attitude Era. For every insult The Great One lobbed in their direction, these rivals had plenty to say in return, and were not afraid to battle for their own place among the WWE elite. To this day, most of them would still get in the ring for a piece of The People's Champ.

CHRIS JERICHO

"I don't give a Brahma Bull's ass what The Rock has to say. Just bring it? Bring what, a vomit bag?"

CHRIS JERICHO

Chris Jericho and The Rock have an entertaining verbal joust (*SmackDown*, October 16, 2001).

It takes considerable gall to interrupt The Rock on your WWE debut, but that is exactly what Chris Jericho did in August of 1999. Jericho revealed himself as the mastermind behind a mysterious countdown clock, which had periodically been ticking down over previous weeks, building tension for Jericho's eventual spectacular appearance, and interrupting a segment hosted by The Rock. The "Millennium Man" clearly aimed to make life miserable for The Rock in the new century. While most other opponents became tongue-tied when The Rock was berating them, Jericho could match his verbal barbs. He was no slouch in the ring, either. Jericho won his first World Title at The Rock's expense, beating him for the WCW Championship at *No Mercy 2001*. Months later, he defeated both The Rock and Stone Cold Steve Austin to become WWE's first Undisputed Champion, his crowning achievement. Despite being thorns in each other's side, The Rock and Jericho have set aside their differences to take on common foes. Both joined Team WWE to vanquish Team Alliance in a critical *Survivor Series* Elimination Match in 2001.

KEN SHAMROCK

Mixed Martial Arts icon Ken Shamrock was as dangerous as The Rock was electrifying. When this hot-tempered competitor snapped, so did somebody's bones. He and The Rock tangled in 1998 as he took out The Rock's Nation teammates one-by-one with an eye toward the Intercontinental Championship.

During Shamrock's WWE career, he was often admonished or even disqualified for losing his cool. The Rock benefited from this reputation twice. At *Royal Rumble 1998*, he planted brass knuckles in Shamrock's tights and framed him for possessing an illegal object. Months later, at *WrestleMania XIV*, Shamrock refused to break his dreaded Ankle Lock submission after The Rock had tapped out, forcing the referee to reverse Shamrock's victory. Learning from his mistake, Shamrock used the same move to beat The Rock and win the 1998 *King of the Ring* tournament.

"You don't have to worry about my temper—Rocky Maivia does."

KEN SHAMROCK

The Rock and Ken Shamrock lock up in the *King of the Ring* tournament finals (*King of the Ring*, June 28, 1998).

A Rock Bottom puts Booker T down for the count (*Unforgiven*, September 23, 2001).

"I'm gonna take his punk ass straight to school!"

BOOKER T

BOOKER T

Booker T was the reigning WCW Champion when WCW closed. He kept his title with him in 2001 when he helped lead the WCW/ECW invasion of WWE. The Rock returned that summer to defend WWE against this insurgence. These two decorated Superstars immediately clashed over their different allegiances and their similar wrestling style. Booker's finishing move, the Bookend, looked just like the Rock Bottom, or vice versa depending on who was talking.

At *SummerSlam 2001*, The Rock won the battle for signature move superiority and, more importantly, the WCW Championship from Booker T. This monumental victory made him the first Superstar to win the WCW Championship at a WWE pay-per-view. Despite a commendable effort to reclaim the title, Booker was unsuccessful, ending up on the receiving end of some of The Rock's most biting insults.

"He called me a jabroni and I'm not gonna stand for that. Does that make me a bad guy?"

BIG SHOW

The first time The Rock met Big Show, the 500-pound behemoth helped him beat Mankind for the WWE Championship. One year later, any goodwill between the two former Corporation members had evaporated. Big Show had a serious case of sour grapes after the 2000 Royal Rumble Match. Video evidence showed that although The Rock had won, his feet had likely touched the floor first as he levered Big Show out of the ring. This controversy put Big Show back in the WWE Title picture, leaving him and The Rock to battle for a spot in the main event of *WrestleMania 2000*.

Unintimidated by his mammoth size, The Rock loved to taunt the giant by mimicking his signature hand gesture and calling him the "Big Slow." The enraged big man was not too slow to dish out some punishing Chokeslams to The People's Champ over the next few years, but was unable to keep him down for long. The Rock eliminated Big Show from the 2001 Royal Rumble Match, further stoking his rage, and leading to another series of heated contests on *RAW* and *SmackDown*.

The Rock builds momentum toward *WrestleMania 2000* in a match against Big Show and Triple H (*RAW*, February 28, 2000).

The Rock attempts to settle a personal grudge with Undertaker (*No Way Out*, February 17, 2002).

The Rock battles Undertaker in his "Big Evil" persona (*No Way Out*, February 17, 2002).

"Everything is a song and dance to The Rock. Well, I don't sing and I don't dance."

UNDERTAKER

UNDERTAKER

Unlike many others, The Rock did not need Undertaker to "make him famous" by facing him, but the journey to the top of WWE always requires a trip through the Deadman's yard. Their first run-ins occurred when The Rock was at odds with the Corporate Ministry, a sinister merger of the Corporation and Undertaker's Ministry. The Rock faced Undertaker in Undertaker's specialty, a Casket Match, and lost. He then challenged Undertaker unsuccessfully for the WWE Championship at *King of the Ring 1999*. Later that year, Undertaker partnered with Big Show, Triple H, Viscera, and others in an attempt to defeat The Rock and Mankind, a.k.a. the popular Rock 'n' Sock Connection.

Despite a short-lived reign as World Tag Team Champions, The Rock and Undertaker were rarely on the same page. The notoriously serious Deadman did not take kindly to the humorous quips that made The People's Champ so beloved, and sought to beat a more respectful tone into his rival. Of course, The Rock refused to stop talking trash. After several heated battles, the two foes nevertheless came to respect each other.

KURT ANGLE

A former Olympic gold medalist, Kurt Angle had it all—intensity, integrity, intelligence—and the talent to thrive in WWE, just as he had in amateur wrestling. Stephanie McMahon even supported Angle over her own husband, Triple H. She was in Angle's corner at *No Mercy 2000*, when Angle defeated The Rock for the WWE Championship. Angle proved the victory was no fluke at *Armageddon*, when he turned back The Rock and four others in a brutal, Six-Man Hell in a Cell Match.

For four months, The Rock tried to earn the title back, only to narrowly miss each time. He finally broke through at *No Way Out 2001*, pinning Angle with a Rock Bottom just in time to carry the gold into WrestleMania X-Seven. Their grudge continued over the next two years. Angle went one on one with The Great One for the WCW and Undisputed Championships, thrilling the WWE Universe with each hard-fought encounter.

> "Rock, you've been jealous of me since the day I stepped into WWE, because finally, there is a man with just as much charisma!"
>
> **KURT ANGLE**

The Rock teams with Lita to win a Mixed Tag Team Match against Kurt Angle and Stephanie McMahon (*SmackDown*, August 24, 2000).

The Rock talks trash to Hulk Hogan weeks before their *WrestleMania X8* clash (*SmackDown*, March 12, 2002).

"All these 'millions and millions of fans,' who were my fans first, are going to see me kick your ass."

HULK HOGAN

HULK HOGAN

In the 1980s, Hulk Hogan and a phenomenon known as Hulkamania swept the sports entertainment world, and WWE became an entertainment powerhouse. When Hogan returned to WWE in 2002 wearing the villainous black-and-white of the New World Order, WWE's modern hero, The Rock, wanted a piece of him at *WrestleMania*. The match not only pitted two icons against each other, but divided the WWE Universe, as many of its older members revered Hogan. The Rock prevailed in this must-see match-up and, in the process, helped Hogan rediscover the heroic values that made him such an 80s sensation. They only shared the ring a handful of times, but The Rock versus Hulk Hogan was always a special rivalry because they each represented their own generation of WWE Superstars and fans.

TRIPLE H

Once cornerstones of rival factions D-Generation X and The Nation of Domination, Triple H and The Rock met again in pursuit of the WWE Championship. By the year 2000, both had established themselves as two of the biggest Superstars. While The Rock was buoyed by the people who chanted his name, Triple H had become a ruthless kingpin, whose cold manipulations had earned him such nicknames as "The Cerebral Assassin" and "The Game." The only people Triple H cared about were those in power. He married Mr. McMahon's daughter Stephanie and together the couple used their family's clout to make sure Triple H remained WWE Champion. While many Superstars fell in line with WWE's power couple, others, like Mankind and The Rock, vowed to bring them down. Unable to get both Superstars fired, Triple H had to settle matters in the ring.

For nearly a year, he and The Rock kept a stranglehold on the WWE Championship, prying the gold from each other's grasp four times. Their most heated confrontation occurred at *Judgment Day 2000*, where they battled in an epic, 60-Minute, Iron Man Match only for The Game to earn the win by disqualification. Weeks later, The Rock pinned Triple H's partner and family patriarch, Mr. McMahon, in a 6-Man Tag Team Match to seize the title without defeating the reigning champ. As their careers unfolded, Triple H and The Rock retained their mutual disdain. Over a decade later, Triple H and Stephanie asserted even greater control over WWE, but this didn't stop The Rock from insulting them at *WrestleMania 31*, just like old times.

"Rock, I am your worst nightmare!"

TRIPLE H

The Rock and Triple H battle in an exhausting 60-Minute Iron Man Match (*Judgment Day* May 21, 2000).

RIVALRIES
JOHN CENA

FOR SEVERAL YEARS, a match between The Rock and John Cena was something the WWE Universe could only dream about. When the dream finally became a reality in 2012, it had become much more than just another match. It was a collision of two generation-defining Superstars with only two things in common— an insatiable drive to succeed and a genuine hatred of each other. Meant to be a "Once in a Lifetime" encounter, fate would lead them to embark upon two clashes that both captivated and divided the WWE Universe.

"When I am on *Monday Night RAW*, Dwayne is on a movie set, sipping a mai tai and laughing at his stunt double."

John Cena

The Rock wants to slap the taste out of John Cena's mouth (*RAW*, February 27, 2012).

Announced as the host of *WrestleMania XXVII*, The Rock returned to WWE for the first time in seven years. He wasted no time sharing his unflattering opinion of the man who had replaced him as WWE's top Superstar—John Cena. His scathing remarks compared Cena to the bowel movements of children's television character Barney the Dinosaur. He also dealt out some humorous one-liners insulting Cena's "You Can't See Me" catchphrase and his brightly colored wardrobe.

The insults escalated over the next several weeks. When The Rock's intervention caused John Cena to lose at *WrestleMania XXVII*, it was clear they needed to settle matters in the ring. Only *WrestleMania* could provide a fitting stage for such a match, so they had to wait until the 28th edition of WWE's grandest event. The war of words became more personal over the next 12 months. Cena slammed The Rock over his decision to leave WWE for Hollywood, while The Rock mocked Cena for his kid-friendly demeanor. Each dipped into his own bag of musical tricks. Cena threw shade in the form of a freestyle rap, while The Rock reprised his "Rock Concert" act, singing brutal barbs as he strummed his guitar.

"You run around here looking like a big, fat bowl of Fruity Pebbles!"

The Rock on John Cena's signature outfits

The Rock mocks John Cena's "You Can't See Me" gesture after landing a Rock Bottom in front of legends Dusty Rhodes and Booker T (*RAW*, March 25, 2013).

After losing the WWE Championship, The Rock shows class by raising John Cena's hand (*WrestleMania 29*, April 7, 2013).

Caught off guard

All talking ceased at *WrestleMania XXVIII* in Miami, Florida, The Rock's hometown. As promised, The Great One brought it to John Cena, looking every bit the champion he was at the turn of the century. Cena was up to the task as well. At one point, it looked like the younger competitor was going to outlast his older rival, but, assuming The Rock was out of energy, Cena made an uncharacteristic mistake. This momentary lapse caused him to walk right into a Rock Bottom. The Rock not only won the match, he devastated Cena in a way that no one else could in Cena's decade-long career. However, both Cena and The Rock were highly respectful to each other after the match. The Rock later commented: "We made history at *WrestleMania*, and we did it for the fans!"

A mutual respect

A year later, Cena blamed The Rock for personal misfortunes that befell him after their match. After Cena won the Royal Rumble Match, The Rock made another miraculous comeback, defeating CM Punk for the WWE Championship. This meant the two icons would not only meet again, but this time WWE's greatest prize would be on the line. Cena achieved redemption at *WrestleMania 29*, defeating The Rock in a main event rematch that saw both men withstand multiple finishing moves. In defeat, The Rock graciously shook the new champion's hand. Each had now owned one hard-fought victory over the other, leaving them with a new feeling of mutual respect.

In later years, these intergenerational rivals have acted civilly toward each other, even forming a brief alliance at *WrestleMania 32*. Both continue to ascend to ever greater heights, each comfortable with his place in history; but with their all-time series tied, the WWE Universe still dreams about a decider!

TIMELINE
THE ROCK VS. JOHN CENA

THE ROCK AND JOHN CENA maintained a fierce rivalry, despite rarely crossing paths. The two icons lobbed verbal grenades at each other via Twitter for over a year before their first match. They also insulted each other on WWE programming, leading to several memorable moments and epic *WrestleMania* encounters.

THE DOCTOR IS IN
RAW: John Cena brings back his rapping "Doctor of Thuganomics" persona from earlier in his career, freestyling some creative rhymes that poke fun at The Rock.

Feb 14, 2011   Feb 20, 2011   Feb 21, 2011   Feb 28, 2011   Mar 7, 2011   Mar 14, 2011

WHERE THE HEART IS
RAW: After seven long years, The Rock finally came home to WWE. The Great One returned to host *WrestleMania*, but first used his inimitable wit to insult WWE's current flagbearer, John Cena.

A SUBTLE RESPONSE
Elimination Chamber: After hearing The Rock compare his fashion style to Fruity Pebbles, John Cena is seen snacking on the sugary cereal.

"YOU RAP TO ME?"
RAW: The Rock is astonished by Cena's gall, responding to him in rap form. He promises that Cena will pay for his remarks.

YOUNG CENA
RAW: With a young child playing the role of "John Cena," The Rock performs a humorous skit, during which he makes the faux Cena seemingly cry by telling him he is simply "not that talented."

THE DOCTOR IS BACK
RAW: Cena doubles down and busts more rhymes at The Rock's expense. He displays a parody of The Rock's "I Bring It" t-shirt.

"YOU STILL GOT IT"

"YOU STILL GOT IT"

Survivor Series: In his first match in over seven years, The Rock is in top form, teaming with Cena to defeat The Awesome Truth. As promised, the partnership ends quickly. After the match, he floors Cena with a Rock Bottom.

FACE TO FACE

RAW: The two adversaries finally meet face to face. Cena's *WrestleMania* opponent, The Miz, interrupts their heated confrontation. The Rock tosses The Miz out of the ring, then Cena blindsides The Rock with an Attitude Adjustment.

THE COUNTDOWN BEGINS

RAW: Both Superstars agree to make history by scheduling a showdown for the next *WrestleMania*. The arrangement sets up an unprecedented full year of anticipation before a main event match.

A LINE IN THE SAND

RAW: With *WrestleMania* approaching, an emotional John Cena talks up his respect for WWE's The Rock and his disdain for the movie star Dwayne Johnson. He vows to win for any other Superstars who choose WWE over the glitz of Hollywood.

Mar, 28, 2011

Apr 3, 2011

Apr 4, 2011

Nov 14, 2011

Nov 20, 2011

Feb 20, 2012

Feb 27, 2012

NEVER BEFORE, NEVER AGAIN

RAW: The Rock accepts John Cena's offer to be his tag team partner at *Survivor Series*. In Cena's hometown of Boston, The Rock warns him that the ceasefire between them will only last one night.

THE PEOPLE'S *WRESTLEMANIA*

RAW: Hosting *WrestleMania XXVII*, The Rock interferes in the WWE Championship Match, hitting Cena with a Rock Bottom and causing him to lose to The Miz.

CHINESE FOOD, ANYONE?

RAW: The Rock assures the WWE Universe of his undying love for WWE and that The Rock and Dwayne Johnson are the same man. He adds that he would like to smack Cena's face "with a handful of kung pao chicken."

ROCKY AND ROCKY

RAW: Philadelphia is the cinematic home of another legendary Rocky, underdog boxing champion Rocky Balboa. Standing beside a statue of the famous character, The Rock wonders how other WWE legends will react to him beating John Cena.

MUSICAL WARFARE

RAW: John Cena delivers another blistering round of hip-hop rhymes. The Rock dusts off his old guitar for a modern "Rock Concert." Spoofing Elvis Presley's "Jailhouse Rock," he derides Cena with sarcastic barbs, making their rivalry even more hostile.

ONCE IN A LIFETIME

WrestleMania XXVIII: In the most anticipated match of all time, The Rock prevails, pinning John Cena with a Rock Bottom.

Mar 12, 2012

Mar 19, 2012

Apr 1, 2012

Mar 5, 2012

Mar 26, 2012

Apr 2, 2012

Jul 23, 2012

JUST THE BEGINNING

RAW: Celebrating his monumental victory at *WrestleMania*, The Rock declares that he is not done and that his goal is once again to become WWE Champion.

HISTORY CLASS

RAW: Once again in Cena's home city of Boston, The Rock tours the city's historical landmarks. At each stop, he disses Cena, at one point hurling his merchandise into the harbor.

LAST WORDS

RAW: On the last episode of *RAW* before *WrestleMania XXVIII*, the two combatants stand face-to-face one more time. The Rock predicts that he will give Cena the beating of a lifetime.

RUMBLE BOUND

RAW: The Rock appears on the 1000th episode of *RAW*. He interrupts a heated conversation between Daniel Bryan and reigning WWE Champion CM Punk to announce that he will be challenging the champion at *Royal Rumble 2012*.

STARS ALIGN

Royal Rumble: The Rock becomes WWE Champion for the first time in ten years by upending CM Punk. That same night, John Cena wins the Royal Rumble Match. This puts Cena on a path to challenge The Rock for the title at *WrestleMania 29*.

Q&A

RAW: A panel of WWE legends grills both competitors about their upcoming rematch. Cena provokes the defending champion into dealing him a Rock Bottom.

OLD SCHOOL *RAW*

RAW: WWE brings back its 1980s set design for a special edition of *RAW*. During a confrontation between *WrestleMania* opponents, The Rock says he only wants to face John Cena because no one else matches his passion and fire.

Jan 27, 2013

Feb 18, 2013

Mar 4, 2013

Mar 25, 2013

Apr 7, 2013

SO LONG SPINNER

RAW: After successfully defending the WWE Championship at *Elimination Chamber*, The Rock overhauls the Championship belt's design. He gets rid of the spinning faceplate that John Cena introduced several years ago and adds Brahma Bull logos to the sideplates.

RESPECT

WrestleMania 29: In a back-and-forth slugfest, John Cena overcomes The Rock for the WWE Championship. As *WrestleMania 29* ends, the two icons shake hands and seem to put their differences aside.

THE ROCK VS. JOHN CENA

WRESTLEMANIA XXVIII 4/1/12

While The Rock was conquering Hollywood, John Cena replaced him as the heroic face of WWE. When The Rock finally returned, the animosity between the two Superstars was instant. Only one Superstar could be considered the best. After a full year of trading personal insults, they finally settled matters in the ring at *WrestleMania*. The dream showdown was hyped as a "Once in a Lifetime" event.

Icons from two generations have a tense stare down before their "Once in a Lifetime" clash.

1: STILL GOT IT

The Miami crowd comes unglued from the start, with a slight majority chanting for their hometown hero, The Rock. He clinches his arms around Cena in a side headlock. Then he takes Cena down with a pair of arm drags, and proves he is as strong and nimble as his younger foe.

2: ROCK IN A HARD PLACE

John Cena injures The Rock's midsection with a powerful bear hug and slams him with an Attitude Adjustment. The Rock shrugs off Cena's onslaught to land a Rock Bottom, only to be caught moments later in the STF submission hold. The pain nearly knocked him unconscious!

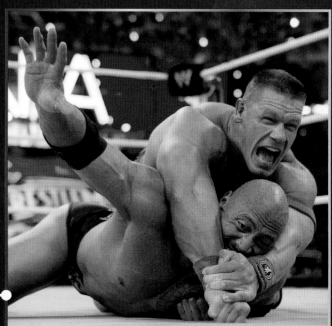

3: DANGER: FALLING ROCKS

The Rock refuses to give up, then equalizes matters with a People's Elbow. The brutal, ground-and-pound contest becomes a stalemate. In desperation, The Rock climbs to the top turnbuckle, a rare sight. He soars through the air and hits Cena with a breathtaking flying crossbody...

4: THE ATTITUDE ERA ADJUSTED

...but Cena is prepared. He uses The Rock's momentum against him, rolling backward into position for another Attitude Adjustment! Somehow, The Rock kicks out just before the three count, leaving Cena aghast. He can't believe anyone would have the fortitude to survive two Attitude Adjustments.

5: ROCK YOU LIKE A HURRICANE

Cena makes a fatal mistake, attempting his own version of the People's Elbow. But out of nowhere, The Rock springs to his feet and stops him with an earth-shaking Rock Bottom and pins him for the three-count. The Rock manages to defend his turf and proves that after eight years away from *WrestleMania*, he was still The Great One.

THE ROCK ARCHIVES

FOR MORE THAN 20 YEARS, The Rock made an unforgettable impression each time he stepped into the ring. Whether headlining a major pay-per-view, battling for WWE supremacy on *RAW*, or thrilling the WWE Universe across the globe, his legacy is chock-full of classic matches. His monumental encounters and hilarious moments are as electrifying as ever every time they are shown on the WWE Network.

Triple H attempts to escape the 15-foot high steel cage, but is thwarted by The Rock (*RAW*, July 5, 1999).

INTERCONTINENTAL CHAMPIONSHIP MATCH
Rocky Maivia vs. Bret "Hit Man" Hart
RAW, March 31, 1997

Only five months into his career, Rocky Maivia defended his Intercontinental Championship against Bret "Hit Man" Hart. Hart was a multitime WWE Champion known as the "Excellence of Execution" for his flawless moves. If the rookie was intimidated by his veteran challenger, Maivia hid it well. The spry up-and-comer showed surprising know-how between the ropes. His athletic Fisherman's Suplex nearly earned him the pin. Failing to get on top, a frustrated Hart got himself disqualified by refusing to break an illegal hold.

Rocky Maivia delivers a textbook Fisherman's Suplex to Bret Hart (*RAW*, March 31, 1997).

STEEL CAGE MATCH
The Rock vs. Triple H
RAW, July 5, 1999

The Rock and Triple H have battled in virtually every type of match. One of their most physical encounters took place in an old-fashioned Steel Cage Match on *RAW*. Triple H's enforcer, Chyna, knocked out the referee and slammed the door on The Rock, enabling Triple H to escape. Because the ref didn't see this, the match continued. The competitors battled until both climbed to the top of the 15-foot cage wall. Triple H fell back into the ring and crawled toward the door. The Rock won, descending the outside of the cage to the floor just before Triple H could exit.

Mr. Ass is manhandled outside the ring by The Rock (*SummerSlam*, August 22, 1999).

KISS MY ASS MATCH
The Rock vs. Mr. Ass
SummerSlam, **August 22, 1999**

Billy Gunn, nicknamed Mr. Ass, often hyped his own hindquarters as being superior to all others. Tired of this cheeky behavior, The Rock battled Gunn in a rare "Kiss My Ass" Match. The rules stated that the loser would have to do as the match title indicated. In victory, The Rock chose to keep The People's Bottom hidden and instead shoved Billy Gunn's face into the backside of a large friend that Gunn had brought to ringside.

NO HOLDS BARRED MATCH
Kane (with Tori) vs. The Rock
SmackDown, **December 30, 1999**

The McMahon-Helmsley faction (Stephanie McMahon and Triple H) spread false rumors that The Rock was ogling Kane's girlfriend, Tori, sending the demon into a jealous rage. Forced into a No Holds Barred Match with one of WWE's most destructive Superstars, The Rock was unfazed. He slowed Kane by knocking him off the *SmackDown* stage through a table. When Tori tried to save her demonic date from a chair attack, she got too close to the action and was accidentally bumped. Kane's concern for her distracted him from The Rock, who promptly dealt him a Rock Bottom for the win.

The Rock refusing to back down to the demonic Superstar, Kane with a threatening glare (*SmackDown*, December 30, 1999).

THE ROCK VS. BIG SHOW
RAW, March 13, 2000

The stakes could not have been higher on the road to *WrestleMania 2000*. The Rock put his career on the line against the 500-pound Big Show for a WWE Championship bid. A win would earn him a place on WWE's ultimate stage, while a loss would earn him The People's Pink Slip. With Big Show's ally Shane McMahon as the self-appointed referee, The Rock's chances looked bleak. Shane favored his pal at every turn until his father, Mr. McMahon, relieved him of his duties. The Rock finished off his super-sized opponent, seizing a spot in *WrestleMania*, saving his career, and earning a three-count from the Chairman himself.

The Rock discards a water bottle before spitting its contents into Big Show's face (*RAW*, March 13, 2000).

TRIPLE THREAT MATCH FOR THE WWE CHAMPIONSHIP
The Rock vs. Triple H vs. Kurt Angle
SummerSlam, August 27, 2000

While Kurt Angle and Triple H were embroiled in a love quarrel over Stephanie McMahon, both men became number one contenders for The Rock's WWE Championship. In a wild Triple Threat Match, Angle was injured crashing through a table, leaving Triple H and The Rock to battle one on one. Stephanie was determined to tilt the odds against The People's Champ. She distracted him at ringside and persuaded Angle to return to the match. In the chaotic finale, Triple H accidentally knocked out his own wife, and Angle laid Triple H low with a sledgehammer. Finally, The Rock hurled Angle out of the ring and pinned the helpless Triple H.

The Rock successfully defends his title by pinning Triple H, accidentally flooring Stephanie McMahon in the process (*SummerSlam*, August 27, 2000).

THE ROCK VS. RIKISHI
Survivor Series, November 19, 2000

The Rock's cousin Rikishi claimed to be an ally, but whether his heart was in the right place was debatable. His attempts to aid The Rock against Kurt Angle at *No Mercy* backfired and cost The Rock the WWE Championship. When The Rock advised harshly to mind his own business, Rikishi became infuriated. All love was lost at *Survivor Series*, where this family fiasco reached a climax. Rikishi mimicked The Rock's new associate, Triple H, and attacked The Rock with a sledgehammer. Undaunted, The Rock disarmed and overcame the 400-pounder for a gutsy victory.

A 400-pound Rock Bottom to Rikishi gives The Rock the upper hand (*Survivor Series*, November 19, 2000)

A Sharpshooter from The Rock weakens his opponent, Chris Jericho (*SmackDown*, April 4, 2002).

THE ROCK VS. JERICHO
SmackDown, April 4, 2002

Selected as *SmackDown*'s number one pick in the first WWE Draft, The Rock dubbed his new home "The People's Show." In his first solo match as a *SmackDown* Superstar, he faced Chris Jericho in the main event. He and Jericho had a history of animosity, and it showed. They brawled on the ramp and in the stands and unleashed a fury of stinging chest slaps. Without the referee seeing, Kurt Angle joined the fray but The Rock survived the two-on-one disadvantage. When order was restored, the Brahma Bull seemed rejuvenated. He quickly pinned his old nemesis to kick off his *SmackDown* era with a flourish.

THE ROCK VS. EDDIE GUERRERO
RAW, July 22, 2002

Eddie Guerrero earned The Rock's ire when he interrupted him on *RAW*, but for Eddie, their issues began much earlier. He was annoyed that his children idolized The Rock and wanted to prove that he was the real hero. Eddie Guerrero was a wily competitor who also came from a famous wrestling family. His smooth, athletic moves offset The Rock's raw power. Eddie escaped a Rock Bottom attempt with a crafty reversal but he could not avoid the People's Elbow. After The Rock deftly avoided a Frog Splash attempt, he struck the decisive blow.

The Rock punishes Eddie Guerrero with Ric Flair's signature move, a Knife Edge Chop to the chest (*RAW*, July 22, 2002).

THE ROCK ARCHIVES

A match worthy of *WrestleMania* happens on *RAW* when The Rock battles Ric Flair (*RAW*, July 29, 2002).

THE ROCK VS. "NATURE BOY" RIC FLAIR
RAW, July 29, 2002

The Rock wanted the honor of facing the incomparable "Nature Boy" Ric Flair in the heart of "Flair Country," Greensboro, North Carolina. The Nature Boy was happy to oblige. In a dream match worthy of *WrestleMania* (or in Flair's heyday, a *Starrcade*), the two legends brought out the best in each other. They traded harsh Knife Edge Chops to the chest, a vintage Flair move, and grueling Figure Four and Sharpshooter leg holds. The Rock defeated the 16-time World Champion in this *RAW* main event; more importantly, he earned his respect.

WWE CHAMPIONSHIP MATCH
The Rock vs. Brock Lesnar vs. Triple H
Global Warning, August 10, 2002

Australian WWE fans anticipate a crowd-pleasing Rock Bottom to manager Paul Heyman (*Global Warning*, August 10, 2002).

The WWE Superstars traveled to Australia for the first time in over a decade. Over 56,000 Aussie fans saw The Rock defend his WWE Championship against both Triple H and Brock Lesnar. The champ survived an early double team by his two mammoth challengers that left him reeling. Then he delighted the crowd by slugging Lesnar's loudmouth manager, Paul Heyman. After Triple H disrupted a pinning attempt by Lesnar, The Rock rewarded him with a Rock Bottom. The WWE Universe down under rejoiced as their hero retained the title to close this historic show.

THE ROCK VS. HULK HOGAN
No Way Out, February 23, 2003

The Rock may have beaten Hulk Hogan at *WrestleMania X8* but the reaction of the WWE Universe told a different story. Hogan received more love from the nostalgic crowd, making The People's Champion feel betrayed. This long-awaited rematch gave The Rock an opportunity to release his pent-up anger. In a bizarre turn of events, the lights went out. When they came back on, Mr. McMahon distracted Hogan. The corrupt referee, who was pretending to be unconscious, slipped The Rock a chair which he used to slug his perplexed opponent, giving the people a real reason to boo.

WWE CHAMPIONSHIP MATCH
The Rock vs. CM Punk
Elimination Chamber, February 17, 2013

CM Punk could not accept losing the WWE Championship to The Rock at *Royal Rumble 2013*. Prior to a rematch at *Elimination Chamber*, the disgruntled Superstar stole the title belt. At first, Punk tried to get The Rock counted out or disqualified, which would have won Punk the title under a special stipulation. When this strategy backfired, Punk went to plan B, the stolen title belt. The Rock alertly ducked as Punk charged with the gold, causing Punk to hit his own manager, Paul Heyman. The Rock then capitalized with a Rock Bottom. This win put The Rock in the main event at *WrestleMania*.

WWE Champion The Rock leaps over CM Punk to set up his Rock Bottom move (*Elimination Chamber*, February 17, 2013).

THE ROCK AT WRESTLEMANIA

IT TAKES A SPECIAL SUPERSTAR to go one on one with The Great One, especially at *WrestleMania*. The Rock helped catapult WWE's cornerstone event to greater heights during the Attitude Era, competing in jaw-dropping main events and cementing his iconic rivalry with Stone Cold Steve Austin. In recent years, he's returned to the Show of Shows in prime condition to deliver dream matches the WWE Universe never thought they would see.

YEAR BY YEAR AT 'MANIA

WRESTLEMANIA 13 (1997):
Rocky Maivia defeats The Sultan to retain the Intercontinental Championship. His father Rocky Johnson helps him turn back a postmatch assault by The Sultan and his followers.

WRESTLEMANIA XIV (1998):
The Rock controversially defeats Ken Shamrock via a Disqualification to retain the Intercontinental Championship. Shamrock originally wins the match, but when he refuses to break his Ankle Lock, the referee reverses the decision.

WRESTLEMANIA XV (1999):
In his first *WrestleMania* main event, The Rock loses the WWE Championship to Stone Cold Steve Austin.

WRESTLEMANIA 2000 (2000):
In a main event Four Way Elimination Match, The Rock (with Vince McMahon) battles Mick Foley (with Linda McMahon), Big Show (with Shane McMahon), and defending WWE Champion Triple H (with Stephanie McMahon). Triple H wins the match when Vince McMahon betrays The Rock.

WRESTLEMANIA X-SEVEN (2001):
In a No Disqualification Match for the WWE Championship, Stone Cold Steve Austin once again beats The Rock for the title. This time, the unthinkable happens: Stone Cold joins forces with Mr. McMahon.

WRESTLEMANIA X8 (2002):
The Rock manages to pin "Hollywood" Hulk Hogan in an entertaining "Icon vs. Icon" Match.

WRESTLEMANIA XIX (2003):
The Rock pins Stone Cold Steve Austin after landing three Rock Bottoms.

WRESTLEMANIA XX (2004):
Evolution (Batista, Ric Flair, Randy Orton) spoil The Rock 'n' Sock Connection's reunion, defeating the popular pair in a 3-on-2 Tag Team Handicap Match.

WRESTLEMANIA XXVII (2011):
The Rock hosts *WrestleMania*. In the main event, he Rock Bottoms John Cena, helping The Miz to victory.

WRESTLEMANIA XXVIII (2012):
The Rock beats John Cena in the main event match hyped for a year as a "Once in a Lifetime" spectacle.

WRESTLEMANIA 29 (2013):
John Cena gets revenge in a rematch, beating The Rock for the WWE Championship.

WRESTLEMANIA XXX (2014):
In the opening segment, The Rock makes a surprise appearance to share an in-ring toast with Hulk Hogan and Stone Cold Steve Austin.

WRESTLEMANIA 31 (2015):
The Rock shows up unannounced to silence Stephanie McMahon and Triple H's gloating, with a little help from Ronda Rousey.

WRESTLEMANIA 32 (2016):
After announcing the record-breaking attendance, The Rock pins Erick Rowan in an impromptu match after 6 seconds, the all-time fastest victory.

The Rock has spent a total of 202 minutes and six seconds in the ring at *WrestleMania*, the sixth most of all time.

In 2011, The Rock became the first-ever host of *WrestleMania*.

The Rock has headlined at five *WrestleManias*, tying for the third most of all time.

The Rock is the only Superstar to beat Hulk Hogan, Stone Cold Steve Austin, and John Cena at *WrestleMania*.

The Rock has taken part in 11 matches at *WrestleMania*.

Shawn Michaels, Undertaker, and The Rock are the only three Superstars to headline *WrestleMania* in three different decades.

The Rock was the defending champion in five of his six championship matches at *WrestleMania*.

The Rock has an impressive *WrestleMania* win-loss record of 6–5.

At *WrestleMania XIX*, The Rock and Stone Cold Steve Austin become the first pairing to compete against each other at three separate *WrestleManias*.

The Rock is tied sixth for the most wins of all time at *WrestleMania*.

The Rock hosts *WrestleMania XXVII* at the Georgia Dome in Atlanta, Georgia (April 3, 2011).

PAY-PER-VIEW

NOW FIXTURES ON the WWE Network, WWE's most popular events are circled on every Superstar's calendar as opportunities to settle their long simmering rivalries. For the bulk of The Rock's career, fans enjoyed these same events on pay-per-view, as The People's Champion strove to check his Attitude Era foes into the SmackDown Hotel. Aside from his impressive record at *WrestleMania*, he also proved himself to be an indelible Superstar in WWE's other three signature events.

SURVIVOR SERIES

It must be something in the crisp November air; the smell of Thanksgiving pie, perhaps. Since making his WWE debut in the 1996 edition, The Rock has feasted in WWE's fall classic, posting a career record of 8-2 at *Survivor Series*. In that inaugural match, his hair might have been questionable, but his talent was not. He stood tall as the "sole survivor," the last Superstar remaining in a traditional *Survivor Series* Match after all other members of both teams had been eliminated. In 2001, he repeated this feat and in the process, saved WWE from a hostile takeover by The Alliance faction.

Not only did The Great One make his WWE debut at *Survivor Series*, he won his first WWE Championship there as well, defeating four Superstars in one night in 1998. The event held such a special place in his heart, he returned to in-ring action at the 2011 version. After seven years of not competing, his skills were so sharp that fans chanted, "You still got it."

ROYAL RUMBLE

Only 24 men (and one woman) can claim a Royal Rumble Match victory on their resume. The Rock is one of them. Entering from the #24 spot, he last eliminated his rival Big Show to etch his name into history. He nearly surpassed himself the following year, lasting a personal best of 38 minutes and 42 seconds in the match, but was tossed out by Kane.

Over his career, The Rock has compiled a respectable 10 eliminations in Royal Rumble Matches, but competing for the WWE Championship has twice kept him out of the namesake match. He brutalized Mankind to win the title in 1999 but fell short in his bid against Chris Jericho in 2002.

SUMMERSLAM

Though his 3-2 career record is bookended by tough losses, The Rock's three-year *SummerSlam* winning streak during his most formative period, 1999-2001, is the perfect cross-section of his career. In those three matches he won the WCW Championship from invading WCW Superstar Booker T, outlasted Triple H and Kurt Angle in a grueling Triple Threat Match to claim the WWE Championship, and rammed Billy Gunn's head into a spectator's dimply rear end. All the fun, action, and irreverence that defined The People's Champ were on display under the summer sun.

The Rock's *SummerSlam* run ended in 2002 at the hands of Brock Lesnar, who proved to be "The Next Big Thing," as advertised. This hard fought encounter marked the only time these two historic Superstars collided on television. A rematch would undoubtedly be an even bigger spectacle that the WWE Universe would love to witness.

The Rock silences cocky Superstar The Miz with a Sharpshooter on the way to victory (*Survivor Series*, November 20, 2011).

OTHER PPV FACTS

The Rock competed in the inaugural *Backlash*, *No Mercy*, *Armageddon*, and *Judgment Day* events.

There have only been seven Iron Man Matches in WWE history. The Rock and Triple H battled in one of them at *Judgement Day* 2000 with Triple H narrowly winning.

In the 1990s, WWE held a series of pay-per-views called *In Your House*. The Rock competed in 14 of the 28 events, including one named after his move: *In Your House: Rock Bottom*.

THE GREAT ONE

WWE SUPERSTARS TALK THE ROCK

"I was super popular, had a lot of great matches, great catchphrases, but I was still always behind The Rock and Steve Austin. I could have lit myself on fire in the middle of the ring and I never would have overtaken the popularity of those two. So if they are the John Lennon and Paul McCartney, I am the George Harrison, or the 'Y2George'of The Attitude Era."

Chris Jericho

"The Rock has transformed WWE and made it into what it is now. Him moving on to Hollywood has brought more attention to our industry and made it cool for people to watch. Back in the day, people were secret wrestling fans and that's not so anymore. The Rock is to thank for that."

Christian

"The Rock has this sing-songy voice that takes the audience along on the ride with them. You know your cue and you are waiting for the catchphrase. It's a fun game as a fan to say, 'Okay, this is my moment. He's going to say his thing and then I come in!' Everything had something to go along with it, a go-to reaction. He led the way with catchphrases to get the crowd involved. I've smelled what The Rock is cooking every single time he's walked through the curtain and I'm sure millions and millions around the world know exactly what I'm talking about."

Trish Stratus

"I think I am actually Rock's favorite person to pick on, because he seems to do it all the time! Aside from that, he is the biggest star to transcend WWE, become a big Hollywood star and not forget his roots. In doing so he has linked two generations. He was very iconic in The Attitude Era with his particular brand of entertainment, and now Rock's evolution is reinvigorating a whole other generation of the WWE Universe. It's great to be a part of."

Stephanie McMahon

"The Rock has paved a road and let Hollywood know WWE Superstars are extremely talented not only in the ring, but outside of it."

Brie Bella

"It is really inspiring how much he has taken over Hollywood because no one thought a WWE Superstar could. It is definitely inspiring and motivating."

Nikki Bella

"A lot of the time I was his foil, the guy he would poke fun at to get the audience to respond. It all came full circle a couple of years ago when we had The Rock's big birthday celebration in Miami, Florida... I got to interact with him in a very entertaining segment. Even though I was Rock Bottomed, it was one of the top highlights of my career."

Michael Cole

"I was only supposed to do one backstage segment with The Rock, but the fans responded to it and things just snowballed. Week after week, we were going at each other with one-liners and zingers with him calling me 'the Hamburglar,' which people still call me to this day. We just had a lot of fun with it. That was complete entertainment for me."

The Hurricane

"Champions aren't born, they are made. If this was easy there would be all kinds of Rocks lining up. Everybody would be buying boots. That's not the case. There's only one Rock and he worked every single night and day for it. I guarantee there were tons and tons of blood, sweat, and tears to get to his level."

Roman Reigns

"The Rock and I were polar opposites. We looked different, we dressed different, we were different. But we had a common goal and that was to entertain. Our rivalry became something bigger than either of us could have imagined and then we became the strangest tag team pairing in WWE history. When people try to name a match we had, it generally stumps them because what they remember is the entertainment. They remember the vignettes, they remember 'This Is Your Life,' they remember our chemistry."

Mick Foley

"After *The Real World*, I was wondering what to do with my life when I looked on a shelf and saw an action figure of The Rock, and I was like, 'I want to be a WWE Superstar.' When Rock came back and was involved with my storyline, it was like every childhood dream come true."

The Miz

"The Rock just has a magnetism and charisma to him that no one else has been able to really touch. He's a guy with a great look, charm, and wittiness. Ladies seem to love him and guys look up to him. Everything about him screams 'star.'"

Big E

"I've had the most amazing interviews with The Rock. It was so hard for me to keep a straight face during a lot of them. One time he looked at me and said, 'You want to be Ms. Rock-cia, don't you?' I blushed and was like, 'Ooh maybe.' We just played off of each other. Of course I'll never forget 'the strudel.' That was born in our interview when he asked if I wanted some of The Rock's 'strudel' and I turned so red. Even now I flush just talking about it!"

Lilian Garcia

❝When you watch somebody compete for the first time you can tell if he is going to rise to the top. Once they gave The Rock the microphone, forget it. Whether he could wrestle or not, he could just say anything and you don't even have to have your eyes open, you know exactly who that voice is. Being in the ring with The Rock brought out the best in me. It was an honor competing against my uso.**❞**

Rikishi

❝I can sum up my rivalry with Dwayne 'The Rock' Johnson by saying it was the biggest emotional, physical, spiritual rollercoaster I have been on in my life.**❞**

John Cena

❝When The Rock was a villain in 1999 he was hard to boo because he was so entertaining. That was during my senior year of high school. Whatever goofy thing he said people would be in school wearing Rock shirts and saying it the next day. He was fun to imitate. Even if he's saying "I hate you!" he would say it in such an entertaining way that it was hard to boo him.**❞**

Daniel Bryan

❝For The Rock, the most memorable thing for me was getting into an argument and him saying to me, 'It doesn't matter what you think!' And the crowd would erupt and go crazy. Just getting that phrase let me know that I made it. It meant that I was in the middle of the game now because if the top guy in the company is telling me 'It doesn't matter what you think,' obviously it must matter.**❞**

Booker T

❝As for what is next for The Rock? Whatever he wants. Whatever avenue he decides to pursue, he is going to be the best at it because that is who he is.**❞**

Triple H

STAYING RING READY

THE ROCK IS admired by millions (and millions) of fans for his energetic and picture-perfect performances in front of cameras, but the real secret to his success is what he does when no one is watching. The Rock's superhero physique is the result of a relentless commitment to training and nutrition. He follows a strict daily regimen that starts the moment he wakes up, and which includes wolfing down seven protein-packed meals per day.

ootball teammates at Miami University once called The Rock "Iron Grip" for his white-knuckled intensity while lifting weights. Decades later, he clings to a bar during a vigorous set of muscle-shredding movements with that same dedication and has been known to occasionally rip his palms open from the effort. The fact that he bleeds might be the only part of The Rock's workouts that reveals that he is, in fact, human. The Rock applies the same intensity to his entire lifestyle, dedicating every waking moment to chasing greatness. Each morning, he gets up around three o'clock to start the day with an intense cardio workout.

On the run

According to The Rock, his presunrise runs get him mentally and physically prepared for the day ahead. At home, The Rock pounds the pavement around his South Florida neighborhood; if he's traveling, he uses an elliptical machine. With wireless headphones and a motivational playlist that includes artists such as Boston, George Thorogood, Kanye West, Kid Rock, NWA, and Tech N9ne, The Rock runs and clears his mind for 30 to 50 minutes. After his workout, The Rock digs into a mountainous breakfast that includes a sirloin steak, eggs, and oatmeal.

Pumping iron

With no directors, photographers, or autograph-seekers to distract him, The Rock escapes to the solitude of the private gym he calls the "Iron Paradise." Surrounded by enough equipment to fill the average public gym, he sculpts some action-movie muscle. Eschewing current fitness fads, The Rock sticks to a tried-and-true bodybuilding routine, focusing on heavy and hard resistance training. He slings cold, old-fashioned steel using strength machines, cables, and free weights, and aims to isolate a different muscle group each day. For most exercises, The Rock completes between four and eight sets of 10 to 20 repetitions, adjusting the weight as needed in order to push his personal limits and follow the age-old weightlifting mantra: "Pain for gain."

Screen-ready

The Rock's workouts are designed for both form and function. They provide the endurance needed for a return match or to meet the demands of a challenging movie role. The Rock recalls "clangin' and bangin'"—his term for aggressive weight training—for eight months to star as the warrior demi-god Hercules in the movie of the same name. To prepare for the role of a firefighter in *San Andreas*, The Rock focused on core training and rope work to hone his physique.

The Rock isolates his biceps inside with a set of preacher curls.

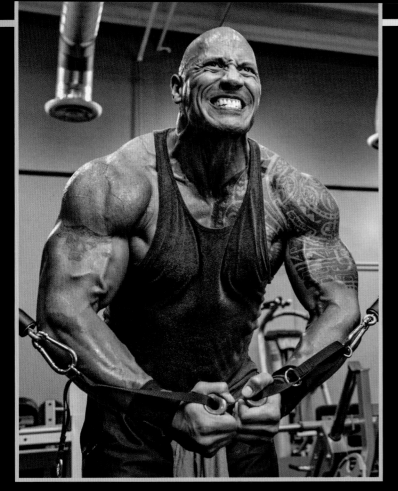
The Rock puts his chest muscles to the test with a Standing cable fly.

One-arm dumbbell rows target The Rock's upper back muscles.

The physical side of The Rock's routine is only half the picture. The Rock's diet is equally important. Depending on the role he is preparing for, The Rock's typical daily intake includes two 10-ounce steaks, two chicken breasts, an eight-ounce salmon, and 13 egg whites. Amazingly, he still has room for copious amounts of vegetables, potatoes, rice, assorted protein shakes, and a salad! To wash it all down, The Rock drinks between two and three gallons of water each day. It is an extremely clean diet, devoid of junk food, but even The Great One allows himself the occasional "cheat day." Once in a while, he'll treat himself to a 12-pancake breakfast and later devour up to four pizzas, several brownies, and other decadent treats. The next day, The Rock resumes his normal discipline.

Appetite for success

Asked what motivates him to keep up such a rigorous routine, The Rock credits the gratitude he feels for his achievements. In 1995, he left home with seven dollars in his pocket. Today, he is a multimillionaire and entertainment icon. Reflecting on this unlikely journey fills him with appreciation and fuels his hunger to build on his success. On The Rock's social media accounts, he shares inspirational workout slogans, such as "together we conquer" and "train to progress," and provides the occasional glimpse inside the "Iron Paradise." By offering a window into his world, The Rock hopes to instill confidence in others to work hard and succeed.

The *Jumanji* Workout

In 2016, The Rock shared the workout for his role as Dr. Bravestone in the film *Jumanji* on the Under Armor Record fitness app. The five-day routine targets back muscles on day one, followed by chest, legs, shoulders, and arms. His grueling routine includes:

Back:
One-arm dumbbell row—3 sets x 12 reps
(pause for 2 seconds at the top)

Chest:
Standing cable fly—7 sets x 15 reps (30 second rest between sets)
Strength machine press—3 sets x 10 reps

Shoulders:
Dumbbell lateral raise—3 sets x 92 reps
(for each set, "run the rack," increasing weight throughout the progression)

Arms:
Skull crushers—3 sets x 8-12 reps
Front double bicep curls—3 sets x 10-15 reps

WHAT IS THE ROCK MADE OF?

MOST PEOPLE WILL never get the chance to be up close and personal with The Most Electrifying Man in Entertainment. For those who do, it is easy to feel intimidated! Standing at six-foot-five and covered in sculpted muscle, The Rock is hard to miss in a crowd. His physique, tattoos, and fierce glare make him one of the most recognizable people in the world.

PETER MAIVIA'S TATTOO

The Rock's grandfather, High Chief Peter Maivia, had tattoos from below his knees up to his abdomen. "His was done old-school style, with a mallet, a little bone and ink..." says The Rock. "The process is incredibly painful and usually takes a month or two." Speaking of the tattoo on his left arm and chest, The Rock explains, "In Polynesian culture, the tattoo means everything to us. My tattoo, just like my grandfather's tattoo, tells a story of our life—our successes, our failures, our loves, and our family." While The Rock's tattoo was applied with more conventional methods, symbolically, the meaning is the same as the High Chief's. "It's a warrior's tattoo," says The Rock.

The section of the tattoo that covers his heart references The Rock's ancestors, the strong women in his family, his baby daughter, his grandfather, and his father, Rocky Johnson.

The Brahma Bull was a core piece of The Rock's identity for two decades. It was a symbol of strength, resilience, heart, power, and defiance. Today, The Rock describes his 25-year-old self as "just a kid" when the bull first graced his beefy arms in 1997.

Despite weighing 260 pounds (118kg), The Rock's waist is a lean 35 inches (89cm) around, compared to his chiseled chest measuring about 50 inches (127cm).

The Rock has always competed in standard wrestling trunks. Since ditching his blue Rocky Maivia trunks in 1997, he has stuck with a black trunk featuring an embroidered logo of his name or the Brahma Bull logo.

Many weightlifters relax their training when it comes to their legs. Not The Rock. His thigh muscles measure about 31 inches, almost as big as his waist.

One of The Rock's many signature threats was to take his size 14 boots and apply them right to an opponent's backside. Of his many phrases to trend worldwide after launching his Twitter account in 2011, "Boots 2 Asses" was one of the most colorful.

NEW INK

In 2017, The Rock chose to cover up his famed Brahma Bull tattoo. After nearly three and a half hours of intricate work by acclaimed tattoo artist Nikko Hurtado, The Rock believes his new tattoo better reflects the man he is today. Through Instagram, he explained the symbolism of its detail: "The cracks and heavy damage in the bone represents life's hard lessons." The horns do not point up or out to the side, but straight ahead, representing relentless energy and forward progress. The Rock explains, "The core and anchor of this image is in the eye. Look closely and you'll find life, energy, and power and you'll feel the MANA (power and spirit, in Polynesian culture). The eye tells the story of a disruptive positive energy always ready to dent the universe."

THE RETURN OF THE ROCK

SINCE HIS FIRST foray into movies as the Scorpion King, The Rock has divided his time between the ring and the silver screen. His thrilling returns to WWE shake up the world of sports entertainment. Whether it has been years, months, or just weeks since they've seen him, the people's reaction can be summed up with one word—FINALLY!

> "Finally, The Rock has come back... home."
>
> **The Rock**

The Rock harshly rejects Shane McMahon's offer to join the anti-WWE group, The Alliance (*RAW*, July 30, 2001).

During his first long hiatus from WWE in 2001, invaders from rival organizations WCW and ECW formed The Alliance. This insurgent faction consisted of many Superstars who had spearheaded a ratings war against WWE, known as *Monday Night War*. To make matters worse, Mr. McMahon's own children, Shane and Stephanie, assumed leadership of the stable, aiming to oust their own father from his perch atop sports entertainment. When The Rock returned, the rogue McMahons lobbied him to join their cause. Fans breathed a sigh of relief as he affirmed his only loyalty was to the WWE Universe. For several months, he helped resist the invasion before ultimately leading Team WWE to victory over Team Alliance at *Survivor Series*, forcing The Alliance to disband.

Courting controversy

His 2003 return did not evoke the same warm and fuzzy feelings, but created drama nonetheless. His controversial defeat of Hulk Hogan had left fans with a sour taste, while his movie career had burgeoned. Once again back in WWE, The Rock disrespected Hogan in interviews and flaunted his crossover success. Every host city witnessed his newfound arrogance as he mocked the audience and local sports teams. He even belittled WWE's resident superhero The Hurricane. Despite the negative vibes, this villainous chapter of The Rock's career had its positive side. It spawned the "Rock Concert," in which The Rock plays amusing songs in the ring as his grandfather had done during his career. It also paved the way for one last match with Stone Cold Steve Austin and a dream match against WCW icon Goldberg.

A renewed connection

By the end of 2003, all was forgiven. While Mick Foley was being attacked on *RAW* by the arrogant tag team La Résistance, the familiar sound of The Rock's entrance sent the crowd into delirium. The two Frenchmen scurried up the ramp, fleeing an impromptu Rock 'n' Sock Connection reunion. Foley knew what to do when facing a similar predicament months later. A target of constant three-on-one assaults by Evolution, Foley called upon his old partner for back-up. A blockbuster match was set for *WrestleMania XX*, where the duo would clash with Foley's three assailants, but first The Rock had some fun. Recalling Foley's iconic 1999 tribute to him, The Rock hosted "Mick Foley, This Is Your Life" on *RAW*, introducing a motley crew of characters from Foley's past.

The Rock is back with less hair and more Hollywood arrogance (*RAW*, March 2003).

The Rock aids his ally Mick Foley by slamming La Résistance tag team member Rob Conway to the mat (*RAW*, December 8, 2003).

The Rock flattens Jonathan Coachman for mistreating the Superstar Eugene (*RAW*, May 17, 2004).

The Rock 'n' Sock Connection fell short in their match at *WrestleMania XX*, but the loss did not discourage The Rock. For the rest of 2004, he emerged whenever a smackdown was needed. He gave one of his most fervent admirers, rookie Superstar Eugene, a vote of confidence and put two of his ardent detractors, The Coach and Randy Orton, in their place. And when WWE needed a host for a Divas' Pie Eating Contest, he made the perfect master of ceremonies. Seeking payback for The Rock's jokes, The Coach tried to spoil the fun, but received a People's Elbow for his pains.

Rocking the crowd

After his run-in with The Coach, The Rock vanished from the ring for seven years, appearing only to induct his father and grandfather into the WWE Hall of Fame Class of 2008, and to address fans from his home on *SmackDown's* tenth birthday. His absence left a void in sports entertainment until he triumphantly strolled down the *RAW* ramp again in February of 2011. His performances on the microphone and in matches with John Cena and CM Punk introduced a new generation to The Great One. Even though he turned 40 in 2012, he looked as ready as ever to dominate WWE.

In January of 2013, he made his first live *SmackDown* appearance in ten years, roughing up The Rhodes Scholars. Days later he performed his third "Rock Concert," aiming his melodious jibes at his prime target, reigning WWE Champion CM Punk. The Rock vowed to become champion again and at *Royal Rumble*, he did, upending Punk to claim the gold for the eighth time and cap an incredible comeback.

The Rock lets Randy Orton know he's heard enough smack talk (*RAW*, June 21, 2004).

The Rock's father Rocky Johnson, grandmother Lia Maivia, and mother Ata Maivia Johnson (WWE Hall of Fame Ceremony, March 29, 2008).

WWE throws Rock a birthday bash in his hometown of Miami, Florida (*RAW*, May 2, 2011).

Since his two-month title reign in 2013, The Rock has shown that wherever his globetrotting lifestyle takes him, WWE will always be home. He has dropped by *RAW* for memorable interactions with The New Day, Rusev, and others. He also appeared at *WrestleMania* events in 2015 and 2016, once alongside MMA star Ronda Rousey and once to announce WWE's record-setting attendance. In appropriate fashion, The Rock broke a record of his own, winning an unexpected match in six seconds, the shortest in *WrestleMania* history. Today, as a new generation of Superstars pursues greatness, those who reach the mountaintop of WWE had better be ready when The Great One decides to lace up his boots one last time.

The Great One interrupts The Authority at *WrestleMania 31* and is joined by MMA star Ronda Rousey.

CHAMPIONSHIP WINS

With 17 separate championship reigns in WWE, The Rock has always brought his best when the stakes are highest. His astounding 10 World Championships, comprising eight WWE and two WCW Titles, make him one of only six Superstars in history to tally double digits on WWE's honors list. While he loves to wow the WWE Universe alone, The Rock has also achieved tag team accolades in his decorated career.

A BRAND-NEW TITLE
RAW: Although The Rock won his second Intercontinental Championship against Stone Cold Steve Austin by forfeit, he bodly claims to be the greatest champion in history and keeps hold of the title for 265 days.

Feb 13, 1997

Dec 8, 1997

Mar 30, 1998

Nov 15, 1998

INTERCONTINENTAL TITLE DEBUT
RAW: The Rock debuts a new title design that lasts nearly fourteen years. The new design features a rounded faceplate and black leather strap.

BEATING A WWE CHAMPION
RAW: A career long rivalry is born when rookie Rocky Maivia unexpectedly defeats the more experienced Triple H for the Intercontinental Championship. Although Triple H dominates most of the match, Maivia refuses to quit. He escapes several pinning attempts en route to winning with a surprise Roll-Up maneuver.

A WIN FOR THE ROCK, AND THE CORPORATION
Survivor Series: The Rock wins the Deadly Game Tournament to claim his first WWE Championship. In the process, he reveals that he's made a backroom deal with Mr. McMahon that ensured his victory, proudly posing with the Chairman after the bell.

A SUCCESSFUL TEAM UP

RAW: Teaming up for the first time, former rivals The Rock and Mankind find instant chemistry, upending Undertaker and Big Show for the World Tag Team Championships.

NO RULES, MEANS NO RULES!

RAW: Although Mankind never truly gives up, as the referee is fooled into believing, The Rock still beats his masked rival. With no rules, The Rock renders Mankind helpless using handcuffs, allowing him to strike at will.

Jan 24, 1999

Feb 15, 1999

Aug 30, 1999

Sep 20, 1999

CLIMBING THE LADDER

RAW: In a Ladder Match against Mankind, The Rock seizes his third WWE Championship and becomes the first Superstar to defeat the same opponent for the title three times.

FACING THE DEADMAN

RAW: Undertaker's demonic henchmen Viscera and Mideon joins Big Show in a "Dark Side Rules" Match where all members of The Ministry of Darkness stable, not just the two announced competitors, can legally participate. The Rock 'n' Sock Connection overcome the evil forces to become two-time Tag Team Champs.

THIRD TAG TITLE REIGN

SmackDown: The Rock 'n' Sock Connection reclaim the titles from The New Age Outlaws who took it away from them weeks earlier. The win puts the unlikely duo in good company among the teams in WWE history with three title reigns.

WALKING THE DARK SIDE

RAW: The Rock and Undertaker rarely see eye to eye, but they enjoy a three-day World Tag Team Championship reign together, winning then losing the titles against Edge and Christian.

Oct 14, 1999

Apr 30, 2000

Jun 25, 2000

Dec 18, 2000

THE ULTIMATE BACKLASH

Backlash: The Rock gains his fourth WWE Title and some sweet revenge against Triple H, who had pinned him at *WrestleMania 2000*.

A WIN AGAINST THE CHAIRMAN

King of the Ring: An unusual Six-Man Tag Team Match is held for the WWE Championship. The tag team set-up means the champion himself does not have to be pinned to lose the title. The Rock takes advantage of the situation by pinning Triple H's teammate, Mr. McMahon, for his fifth Championship reign.

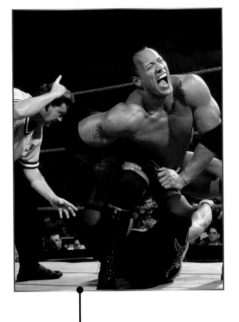

WCW CHAMPION

RAW: Days after his short-lived truce with Jericho to capture the tag team titles, The Rock refocuses on his original goal, becoming a two-time WCW Champion. To do so, he ousts his ex-partner in a match on *RAW*.

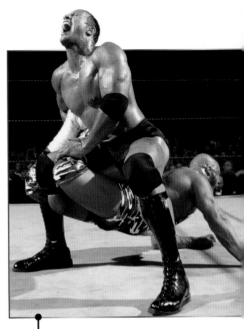

SIX-TIME CHAMPION

No Way Out: Facing the man who ended his fifth reign, Kurt Angle, The Rock gains some notoriety by besting Angle to become the first-ever six-time WWE Champion.

A SEVENTH WIN

Vengeance: The Rock's record-setting seventh WWE Championship is made more impressive by defeating both Kurt Angle and Undertaker in a Triple Threat Match.

Feb 25, 2001

Aug 19, 2001

Oct 22, 2001

Nov 5, 2001

Jul 21, 2002

Jan 27, 2013

BOOKER T LOSES THE CHAMPIONSHIP

SummerSlam: Hall of Famer Booker T famously held the WCW Championship five times. It is The Rock who ends his fifth and final reign, stealing the WCW Title from The Alliance stable member.

A WINNING PAIR

RAW: Chris Jericho had just beaten The Rock for the WCW Title the previous night, yet the bitter rivals put harsh feelings aside to beat The Dudley Boyz in a tag team match. The win marks The Rock's fifth World Tag Team Title.

THE ROCK ON TOP

Royal Rumble: As Mr. McMahon tries to strip CM Punk of the WWF Championship for cheating, The Rock cuts him off and instead, demands their hard-hitting match be restarted. Unfazed, The Rock decks Punk with a People's Elbow. After ten long years, The Great One delivers on his promise to bring the title home for the eighth time.

THE ROCK IN HOLLYWOOD

THE ROCK was not the first WWE Superstar to branch out into the broader world of entertainment, but he is by far the most successful. Having graced *Forbes'* "The World's Highest-Paid Actors" list multiple times, even topping it as recently as 2016, he is living the dream of anyone with Hollywood aspirations. A perennial powerhouse of all screens, big and small, The Rock is as hot a commodity as any actor of his generation, compiling high-profile roles and awards faster than he collected titles in WWE. Movies in which he has acted have pulled in a whopping total of $9.2 billion combined in gross revenue, with starring roles accounting for nearly half that amount.

As his star rose in WWE in the late 1990s, The Rock began to make brief TV appearances. In That '70s Show, broadcast on February 7, 1999, he had a cameo as his own father, Rocky Johnson; while in the "Tsunkatse" episode of *Star Trek: Voyager*, aired on February 9, 2000, he played a Pendari warrior. On March 18 that same year, he hosted *Saturday Night Live*, taking a variety of hilarious roles and also showing off his singing voice. He crooned "Are You Lonesome Tonight?" flanked by WWE Superstars Mick Foley and Big Show. No wonder Hollywood producers reached for the telephone, eager to bring The Rock to the silver screen. "*SNL* was an amazing opportunity for the world to see that WWE is a great space to be in terms of live performance," The Rock commented.

DWAYNE JOHNSON

The Rock's character Mathayas uses his bow and arrow to save a young boy from the villain Memnon's guards (*The Scorpion King*, 2001).

"It opened a lot of doors for me and it afforded many opportunities down the road for a lot of other guys. That's what you want, to leave your footprint and your legacy in a business you helped evolve, and create opportunities for others to shine."

The Rock's grandfather, Peter Maivia, had previously appeared as a heavy in the 1967 James Bond film, *You Only Live Twice*. The Rock, however, had much bigger plans. Having laid the groundwork, he made his movie debut in the 2001 film *The Mummy Returns*. He then reprised his role the following year as the title character in the prequel, *The Scorpion King*. Though his mainstream takeoff had barely left the runway, many observers saw no limits to his ascension. The famed Madame Tussauds wax museum agreed. On April 10, 2002, The

Rock was officially immortalized as a wax statue in their renowned New York City museum, joining the likes of Marilyn Monroe, Bruce Willis, and Michael Jackson. The statue depicted him in his most recent WWE gear at that time, with his glitzy gold Brahma Bull belt buckle, leather vest, and of course, a permanent People's Eyebrow raised at his admirers. The prestigious honor only motivated The Rock to prove himself worthy.

The Rock poses in his role as his dad, Rocky Johnson, on *That '70s Show*.

The Rock poses with his waxwork figure (Madame Tussauds Wax Museum, April 10, 2002).

His performances opened doors to a wide range of opportunities. The wholehearted way he tackled each role proved he had real talent. As Beck in the 2003 movie *The Rundown*, moviegoers began to regard him as a genuine action star. Following up with dramatic roles in *Walking Tall* (2004), *Gridiron Gang* (2006), and comedic roles in *Be Cool* (2005) and *The Game Plan* (2007), emphasized his considerable range. He no longer needed to rely on his WWE persona and starred as Dwayne Johnson. Nevertheless, despite his distance from WWE during this time, he always credited the company as the springboard for his meteoric success. "Coming from the world of WWE... forces you to become a great performer. I always say there was no greater place for me to cut my teeth than in this environment."

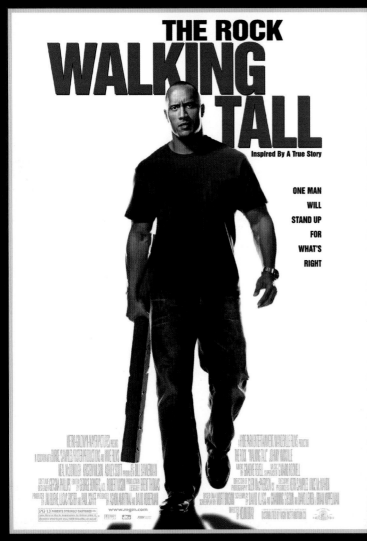

Theatrical release poster for *Walking Tall* (2004).

Fresh from the popular 2009 action-adventure film *Race to Witch Mountain*, Dwayne Johnson once again graced *Saturday Night Live* as "The Rock Obama," a superhuman alter ego of United States President Barack Obama. Having lampooned the incumbent president, Hollywood's most prominent tough

guy played against type as "The Tooth Fairy." Later used as ammunition for John Cena to poke fun at him, the ironic sight of Dwayne Johnson in a tutu was comedy gold, and revealed his self-deprecating sense of humor. He delivered more laughs in 2010's *The Other Guys*—which marked the beginning of a successful decade in Hollywood.

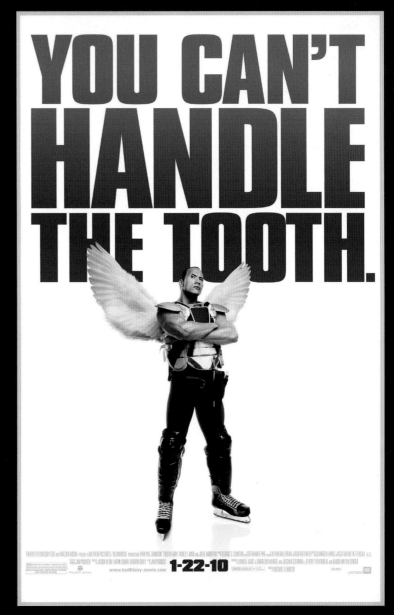

Theatrical release poster for *The Tooth Fairy* (2010).

In 2011, Dwayne joined long-time friend Vin Diesel and the late Paul Walker in *The Fast And The Furious* franchise. Its fifth instalment, *Fast Five*, unveiled his character, Hobbs, a determined federal agent pursuing a rogue group of racers. Adding even more star power took the blockbuster franchise to greater heights, and Hobbs became a central figure in three sequels, culminating in 2017's *The Fate of the Furious*. Today, the name Hobbs is proudly carried on by The Rock's pet French bulldog. "The great thing about making movies is you have the opportunity to have massive success and a big franchise, take ownership of it, prepare for it, and work your ass off for it," says Johnson. After a decade of hard

Theatrical release poster for *Fast and Furious 5* (2011).

work in many genres, he had become a franchise star and Tinseltown's hottest property. In 2013, The Rock graced the silver screen in five movies, with filmgoers spending a total of $1.3 billion to see him—more than any actor in the world. Ever since, he has ranked among the elite each year, attracting droves of fans to the box office. What made The Rock's boost in popularity even more special is the fact it extended across all ages. His performance in *Journey 2: The Mysterious Island* earned him the Nickelodeon Kids' Choice Award for "Favorite Male Buttkicker." To close the jubilant award show, he took part in a popular Nickelodeon tradition: getting doused with massive amounts of neon green slime. In a night highlighted by slimings of stars such as Neil Patrick Harris, Sandra Bullock, and Pitbull, The Rock's was the biggest of the night. For good measure, he lured in the show's hosts Nick Cannon and Josh Duhamel to get a taste of the goo themselves.

Johnson followed up his impressive 2013 with what he considered the role of a lifetime as the title character in *Hercules*. Playing the son of Zeus required him to amp up his

legendary workouts. Swinging the demigod's battle club with otherworldly muscle, he redefined this iconic character—a feat that has become one of his great talents. Johnson also breathed new life into pop culture favorites such as *GI Joe: Retaliation* (2013), *Baywatch* (2017), and *Jumanji: Welcome to the Jungle* (2017). His performance in the latter as Dr. Bravestone helped catapult the flick into the record books as the highest domestic grossing film ever for Sony Pictures. He followed up this smash hit with another larger-than-life performance. In the 2017 movie *Rampage*, The Rock stopped an oversized, mutated primate named George from destroying Chicago.

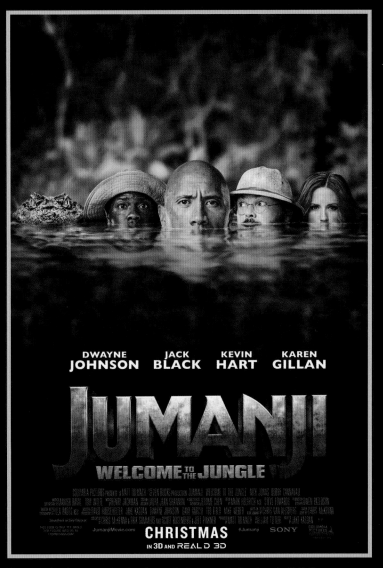
Theatrical release poster for *Jumanji: Welcome to the Jungle* (2017).

The Rock attends the premiere of *Journey 2: The Mysterious Island* (2012).

In 2015, Johnson produced and starred in his own HBO television series—*Ballers*. A nod to his early life and his love of football, the series follows Dwayne's character Spencer Strasmore, a retired NFL player-turned manager. Featuring real-life NFL players, the show explores the chaotic lifestyles of professional athletes, and tackles many relevant issues in modern sports with an energetic blend of drama and comedy. In 2017, HBO announced that this popular show would return for an impressive fourth season.

tattoos, Johnson's character Maui resembles a combination of himself and his grandfather, High Chief Peter Maivia. What really tugged Johnson's heartstrings, however, was the fact that the film's young heroine reminded him of his own teenage daughter. As he told *ABC News*: "[She is] ambitious and has a really strong point of view. Wants to tackle the world." Moana is no "damsel in distress," something Johnson finds empowering for young women everywhere, including his daughter. "I have never cried consistently... through a movie more than I have with this movie," Johnson said. "Just to be clear, they're all manly tears, though."

Manly tears flowed once again on December 13, 2017, when Dwayne Johnson was given his own star on the Hollywood Walk of Fame. Joining the all-time greats of entertainment on the iconic street, he expressed his gratitude to the many friends and family members that had helped him along the way. This prestigious award brought his career full circle, but he has no intention of slowing down. As his new Brahma Bull tattoo symbolizes, Dwayne keeps charging ahead, and is poised for greater challenges and success in the years to come.

The Rock attends the premiere of *Rampage* (2017).

At the same time, news broke that Dwayne would be a Producer for a biopic entitled *Fighting with My Family*, based on the true story of WWE Superstar Paige and her family. Inspired by a British documentary, the movie tracks the struggles of the wrestling family. As Paige's parents, Ricky and Julia, seek a better life for their children, the brother and sister attempt to fulfill their WWE dreams. As they learn the rigors of becoming a WWE Superstar, it brings the family closer together and also threatens to tear it apart. Johnson, who makes a cameo as himself, can relate. Speaking of the film, he says, "The Knights' journey is a universal one that all families are familiar with. I relate to Saraya (Paige) and her wrestling family on such a personal level and it means so much that I can help tell their story."

While crafting his ground-breaking TV series and preparing for another round of starring roles, Johnson lent his voice to Disney for the 2016 animated film *Moana* set in the Polynesian pacific. With a stocky build, wavy hair, and tribal

The Rock in his role as Producer on *Fighting with My Family* (2017).

In 2019, the *Jumanji* star returns to the wilderness, this time aboard a tour boat in Disney's *Jungle Cruise*. Based on the popular theme park ride, the film sets a group of passengers on a perilous adventure along the Amazon River. During the summer, *Fast and the Furious* fans will welcome his character Hobbs back to the silver screen. In a spin-off of the '*Furious* franchise titled *Hobbs and Shaw*, Johnson's character finds an unlikely ally in his old rival, Deckard Shaw, played by Jason Statham. Amidst all the action and adventure, Dwayne will also earn his superhero stripes. Following his work as an Executive Producer in the upcoming DC Comics movie *Shazam!*, he will suit up as the title character in the movie *Black Adam* and star as the diabolical anti-hero. Not to be slowed down by these otherworldly pursuits, The Rock will also begin work producing and starring in Universal's *Red Notice* movie beginning in April of 2019.

The Rock's memory of leaving home with seven dollars in his pocket in 1995 has inspired the name of his production company—Seven Bucks Productions—where he continues to pioneer new ideas for television, film, and digital networks. If there is a corner of the entertainment world that he has not yet electrified, The Rock will relentlessly pursue it, letting nothing stand in his way.

Dwayne 'The Rock' Johnson has his hands and footprints immortalized at the famous TCL Chinese Theater IMAX (Los Angeles, California May 20, 2015).

INDEX

Page numbers in **bold** refer to the main pages for the entry.

DK | Penguin Random House

Project Editor Pamela Afram
Senior Designer Nathan Martin
Proofreader Kayla Dugger
Pre-Production Producer Marc Staples
Producer Lloyd Robertson
Managing Editor Paula Regan
Managing Art Editor Jo Connor
Art Director Lisa Lanzarini
Publisher Julie Ferris
Publishing Director Simon Beecroft

Global Publishing Manager Steve Pantaleo
Vice President, Consumer Products Sylvia Lee
Executive Vice President, Consumer Products Casey Collins
Vice President — Photography Bradley Smith
Photo department Josh Tottenham, Frank Vitucci,
Georgiana Dallas, Jamie Nelson, Melissa Halladay, Mike Moran
Senior Vice President, Assistant General Counsel—Intellectual Property
Lauren Dienes-Middlen
Senior Vice President, Creative Services Stan Stanski
Creative Director John Jones
Project Manager Sara Vazquez

Dorling Kindersley would also like to thank Helen Peters for the index;
Alastair Dougall and Hannah Gulliver-Jones at DK for editorial assistance;
Anna Pond and Rhys Thomas at DK for design assistance.

First American Edition, 2018
Published in the United States by DK Publishing
345 Hudson Street, New York, New York 10014

Page design copyright ©2018 Dorling Kindersley Limited
DK, a Division of Penguin Random House LLC
18 19 20 21 22 10 9 8 7 6 5 4 3 2 1
001–309510–Oct/2018

DK books are available at special discounts when purchased in bulk
for sales promotions, premiums, fund-raising, or educational use.
For details, contact: DK Publishing Special Markets
345 Hudson Street, New York, New York 10014
SpecialSales@dk.com

Photograph on page 146 courtesy of Pro Wrestling Illustrated.
Photography on pages 140-141 by Perbernal.com.
Photograph on page 157 courtesy of Erich Charbonneau_Invision_Warner Bros_AP Images.

The publisher would like to thank the following for their kind permission to reproduce
their photographs: (key: a-above; b-below/bottom; c-centre; f-far; l-left; r-right; t-top)
p.152 Rex by Shutterstock: Eric Charbonneau (r). p.154 Rex by Shutterstock: Foxvan Prods.
/ Kobal (cr); Mandeville / Hyde Park / Kobal (clb). p.155 Rex by Shutterstock: Columbia
/ Sony / Kobal (cr); Snap Stills (tl). p.156 Rex by Shutterstock: Eric Charbonneau (tl)

All other images © Dorling Kindersley
For further information see: www.dkimages.com

Printed and bound in China

A WORLD OF IDEAS:
SEE ALL THERE IS TO KNOW

www.dk.com
www.wwe.com